New American Haggadah

Edited by Jonathan Safran Foer
With a new translation by Nathan Englander

Designed by Oded Ezer

Commentaries by Nathaniel Deutsch ("House of Study")
Jeffrey Goldberg ("Nation")
Rebecca Newberger Goldstein ("Library")
Lemony Snicket ("Playground")

Timeline created by Mia Sara Bruch

LITTLE, BROWN AND COMPANY
New York | Boston | London

Little, Brown and Company
Hachette Book Group
237 Park Avenue, New York, NY 10017
www.hachettebookgroup.com

First Edition: March 2012

Little, Brown and Company is a division of Hachette Book
Group, Inc., and is celebrating its 175th anniversary in
2012. The Little, Brown name and logo are trademarks of
Hachette Book Group, Inc.

The publisher is not responsible for websites (or their
content) that are not owned by the publisher.

Library of Congress Cataloging-in-Publication Data
Haggadah. English & Hebrew.
  New American Haggadah / edited by Jonathan Safran
Foer ; with a new translation by Nathan Englander ;
designed by Oded Ezer ; commentaries by Nathaniel
Deutsch ("House of Study") ... [et al.] ; timeline created
by Mia Sara Bruch.
     p. cm.
  ISBN 978-0-316-06986-1
  1. Haggadot—Texts. 2. Seder—Liturgy—Texts. 3.
Judaism—Liturgy—Texts. 4. Haggadah. I. Foer, Jonathan
Safran, 1977- II. Englander, Nathan. III. Ezer, Oded. IV.
Deutsch, Nathaniel. V. Bruch, Mia Sara. VI. Title.
  BM674.643F64 2012
  296.4'5371—dc23   2011040637

10 9 8 7 6 5

Printed in the United States of America

WOR

THIS HAGGADAH

ere we are. Here we are, gathered to celebrate the oldest continually practiced ritual in the Western world, to retell what is arguably the best known of all stories, to take part in the most widely practiced Jewish holiday. Here we are as we were last year, and as we hope to be next year. Here we are, as night descends in succession over all of the Jews of the world, with a book in front of us.

Jews have a special relationship to books, and the Haggadah has been translated more widely, and reprinted more often, than any other Jewish book. It is not a work of history or philosophy, not a prayer book, user's manual, timeline, poem, or palimpsest—and yet it is all of these things. The Torah is the foundational text for Jewish law, but the Haggadah is our book of living memory. We are not merely telling a story here. We are being called to a radical act of empathy. Here we are, embarking on an ancient, perennial attempt to give human life—*our lives*—dignity.

The need for new Haggadahs does not imply the failure of existing ones, but the struggle to engage everyone at the table in a time that is unlike any that has come before. Our translation must know our idiom, our commentaries must wrestle with our conflicts, our design must respond to how our world looks and feels. This Haggadah makes no attempt to redefine what a Haggadah is, or overlay any particular political or regional agenda. (It is called *New American Haggadah* not because there is anything uniquely American about it, but in the tradition of naming a Haggadah after where it was made.) Like all Haggadahs before it, this one hopes to excite the mind and heart. Like all Haggadahs before it, this one hopes to be replaced.

Here we are: Individuals remembering a shared past and in pursuit of a shared destiny. The seder is a protest against despair. The universe might appear deaf to our fears and hopes, but we are not— so we gather, and share them, and pass them down. We have been waiting for this moment for thousands of years—more than one hundred generations of Jews have been here as we are—and we will continue to wait for it. And we will not wait idly.

As you read these words—as our people's ink-stained fingers turn its wine-stained pages—new Haggadahs are being written. And as future Jews at future tables read *those* Haggadahs, other Haggadahs will be written. New Haggadahs will be written until there are no more Jews to write them. Or until our destiny has been fulfilled, and there is no more need to say, "Next year in Jerusalem."

New American Haggadah

בָּרוּךְ אַתָּה יהוה, אֱלֹהֵינוּ מֶלֶךְ הָעוֹלָם, אֲשֶׁר קִדְּשָׁנוּ בְּמִצְוֹתָיו, וְצִוָּנוּ
עַל בִּעוּר חָמֵץ.

כָּל חֲמִירָא וַחֲמִיעָא דְּאִכָּא בִרְשׁוּתִי, דְּלָא חֲמִיתֵּהּ וּדְלָא בַעַרְתֵּהּ, וּדְלָא
יְדַעְנָא לֵהּ, לִבָּטֵיל וְלֶהֱוֵי הֶפְקֵר כְּעַפְרָא דְאַרְעָא.

כָּל חֲמִירָא וַחֲמִיעָא דְּאִכָּא בִרְשׁוּתִי, דַּחֲמִיתֵּהּ וּדְלָא חֲמִיתֵּהּ, דְּבַעַרְתֵּהּ
וּדְלָא בַעַרְתֵּהּ, לִבָּטֵיל וְלֶהֱוֵי הֶפְקֵר כְּעַפְרָא דְאַרְעָא.

יְהִי רָצוֹן מִלְּפָנֶיךָ יהוה אֱלֹהַי וֵאלֹהֵי אֲבוֹתַי, שֶׁכְּשֵׁם שֶׁאֲנִי מְבָעֵר/מְבַעֶרֶת
חָמֵץ מִבֵּיתִי וּמֵרְשׁוּתִי כֵּן אֶזְכֶּה לְבַעֵר אֶת יֵצֶר הָרַע מִלִּבִּי, וְכֵן תְּבַעֵר
אֶת כָּל הָרִשְׁעָה מִן הָאָרֶץ.

Removal of the Hametz

On the night preceding the first night of Passover, search the house for any remaining hametz. (If Passover begins Saturday night, search on Thursday night.) The custom is to hide ten morsels of hametz throughout the house and then to search for them by candlelight. Before beginning the search, say:

You are blessed, Lord God-of-Us, King of the Cosmos, who has set us apart with his mitzvot, and instructed us to eliminate all hametz.

After all ten pieces are found, sweep them up with the help of a feather and wooden spoon. Collect them and say:

All hametz in my domain—both rising and risen—that I have failed to see and failed to eliminate, and of which I was left unaware, may it be annulled and made ownerless, as free for all as the dust of the earth.

Wrap up the searching utensils (candle, feather, spoon) with the hametz, secure, and set aside. The following early morning, burn the collected hametz and any other remaining hametz. As it burns, say:

All hametz in my possession—both rising and risen—that which I have seen and that which I have failed to see, that which I eliminated and which I failed to eliminate, may it be annulled and made ownerless, as free for all as the dust of the earth.

Just as I have eliminated the hametz from my house and from all I possess, may it be desirous before you, the One Who Brings Being into Being, God to me and God to my fathers, to rid me of the Evil Inclination; may I be privileged enough to have that urge burnt from the depths of my heart until it is no more than smoke. And so too may you, like the very wind of destruction, rid by fire all the wickedness from the land.

הדלקת נרות

בָּרוּךְ אַתָּה יהוה, אֱלֹהֵינוּ מֶלֶךְ הָעוֹלָם, אֲשֶׁר קִדְּשָׁנוּ בְּמִצְוֹתָיו, וְצִוָּנוּ לְהַדְלִיק נֵר שֶׁל [שַׁבָּת וְשֶׁל] יוֹם טוֹב.

בָּרוּךְ אַתָּה יהוה, אֱלֹהֵינוּ מֶלֶךְ הָעוֹלָם, שֶׁהֶחֱיָנוּ וְקִיְּמָנוּ וְהִגִּיעָנוּ לַזְּמַן הַזֶּה.

עריכת שולחן הסדר

Candle Lighting

Before sunset, light candles near where the seder will be held. Then, while covering one's eyes, recite the blessing (on Friday afternoon, add the words in brackets):

You are blessed, Lord God-of-Us, King of the Cosmos, who has set us apart with his mitzvot, and instructed us to ignite a [Shabbat and] festival light.

You are blessed, Lord God-of-Us, King of the Cosmos, who breathed life, and sustained life, and shepherded us through to the current season.

Preparing the Seder Table

Once night falls, prepare the holiday table for the seder. As befitting "free men," set the dining table in the most regal manner, displaying the finest utensils, with a cushion at each seat for reclining. Upon the table, prepare the seder plate in the following manner:

Cover a stack of three whole matzot under a cloth, or beneath the seder plate. Arrange the following symbolic food items on the seder plate:
Upper right: Zeroa—a broiled piece of meat bone, such as a shank bone or chicken neck.
Upper left: Betzah—a hard-boiled egg.

Between these: Maror—some horseradish and/or bitter lettuce, such as romaine.
Lower right: Charoset—a sweet mixture of chopped nuts, fruits, and wine.
Lower left: Karpas—A (root) vegetable for dipping, such as onion, parsley, or potato.
Between these: Chazeret—as with maror, some horseradish, and/or bitter lettuce.

Place a wine cup at each setting. On the table there should also be: a (broken) bowl with salt water, a large goblet in honor of Elijah the Prophet, extra matzot, and the other ceremonial foods.

The telling begins sometime between 1250 and 1200 BCE, when a document known to archaeologists as "Papyrus Anastasi V" reports that slaves have escaped from a palace at Pi-Ramesses into the Sinai. In 1213, Pharaoh Ramesses the Great, renowned for his military victories and believed to be the Pharaoh of the Exodus, dies. Around 1100, the first forms of Hebrew literature take shape, including the "Song at the Sea" (Exodus 15:21) celebrating God's destruction of the Egyptian army as the Israelites fled to freedom:

I will sing to the Lord, for He has triumphed gloriously Horse and driver he has hurled into the sea.

Once everything is set, chant:

Let us...

Sanctify	קַדֵּשׁ
And Wash	וּרְחַץ
Dip	כַּרְפַּס
Split	יַחַץ
And Tell	מַגִּיד
Be Washed	רָחְצָה
And Bless	מוֹצִיא
The Poor Man's Bread	מַצָּה
Bitter	מָרוֹר
Bundle	כּוֹרֵךְ
And Set Down to Eat	שֻׁלְחָן עוֹרֵךְ
Hide It	צָפוּן
And Bless	בָּרֵךְ
Praise It	הַלֵּל
Be Pleased	נִרְצָה

Tonight, Ramesses'
mummy is in the
Cairo Museum,
and the papyrus
document reporting
the escape of the
slaves is in the
archives of the
Jewish Theological
Seminary in New
York City. Tonight,
3,000 years later, we
are here.

WAR

כּוֹס רִאשׁוֹן

קַדֵּשׁ

הִנְנִי מוּכָן/מוּכָנָה וּמְזֻמָּן/וּמְזֻמֶּנֶת
לְקַיֵּם מִצְוַת כּוֹס רִאשׁוֹן
שֶׁהוּא כְּנֶגֶד בְּשׂוֹרַת הַיְשׁוּעָה
שֶׁאָמַר הַקָּדוֹשׁ בָּרוּךְ הוּא לְיִשְׂרָאֵל:
וְהוֹצֵאתִי אֶתְכֶם מִתַּחַת
סִבְלוֹת מִצְרָיִם.

[וַיַּרְא אֱלֹהִים אֶת כָּל אֲשֶׁר עָשָׂה וְהִנֵּה טוֹב
מְאֹד, וַיְהִי עֶרֶב וַיְהִי בֹקֶר יוֹם הַשִּׁשִּׁי.
וַיְכֻלּוּ הַשָּׁמַיִם וְהָאָרֶץ
וְכָל צְבָאָם. וַיְכַל אֱלֹהִים בַּיּוֹם
הַשְּׁבִיעִי מְלַאכְתּוֹ אֲשֶׁר עָשָׂה, וַיִּשְׁבֹּת בַּיּוֹם
הַשְּׁבִיעִי מִכָּל מְלַאכְתּוֹ אֲשֶׁר עָשָׂה.
וַיְבָרֶךְ אֱלֹהִים אֶת יוֹם הַשְּׁבִיעִי וַיְקַדֵּשׁ
אֹתוֹ, כִּי בוֹ שָׁבַת מִכָּל מְלַאכְתּוֹ אֲשֶׁר בָּרָא
אֱלֹהִים לַעֲשׂוֹת.]

סַבְרִי מָרָנָן וְרַבָּנָן וְרַבּוֹתַי:
בָּרוּךְ אַתָּה יהוה
אֱלֹהֵינוּ מֶלֶךְ הָעוֹלָם
בּוֹרֵא פְּרִי הַגָּפֶן.

בָּרוּךְ אַתָּה יהוה אֱלֹהֵינוּ מֶלֶךְ
הָעוֹלָם אֲשֶׁר בָּחַר בָּנוּ מִכָּל עָם
וְרוֹמְמָנוּ מִכָּל לָשׁוֹן וְקִדְּשָׁנוּ בְּמִצְוֹתָיו.
וַתִּתֶּן לָנוּ יהוה אֱלֹהֵינוּ בְּאַהֲבָה [שַׁבָּתוֹת
לִמְנוּחָה וּ]מוֹעֲדִים לְשִׂמְחָה, חַגִּים וּזְמַנִּים
לְשָׂשׂוֹן, אֶת יוֹם [הַשַּׁבָּת הַזֶּה וְאֶת
יוֹם] חַג הַמַּצּוֹת הַזֶּה, זְמַן
חֵרוּתֵנוּ, [בְּאַהֲבָה] מִקְרָא קֹדֶשׁ, זֵכֶר
לִיצִיאַת מִצְרָיִם.
כִּי בָנוּ בָחַרְתָּ וְאוֹתָנוּ קִדַּשְׁתָּ
מִכָּל הָעַמִּים, [וְשַׁבָּת] וּמוֹעֲדֵי קָדְשֶׁךָ
[בְּאַהֲבָה וּבְרָצוֹן] בְּשִׂמְחָה וּבְשָׂשׂוֹן
הִנְחַלְתָּנוּ. בָּרוּךְ אַתָּה יהוה מְקַדֵּשׁ
[הַשַּׁבָּת וְ]יִשְׂרָאֵל וְהַזְּמַנִּים.

First Cup

Kadesh

Fill the cup with wine, rise, and reflect:

Here I am, prepared and ardent, allied and present, ready to perform the mitzvah of the first cup, the enactment of salvation's promise. As the Holy One, Blessed is He, declared to Israel: *And I will lift you out from under the millstone that is Egypt.*

Raise the cup and recite (on Friday night, add the words in brackets):

[And God reviewed the whole of what he had done and, behold, it was a wonder. And evening went by and morning went by, constituting the sixth day. And the skies and the earth and all their legions reached their peak. And on the seventh day God had completed the labor of what He had done, and He settled on the seventh day from *all* the labor of what He had done. And God blessed that seventh day and distinguished it in holiness, because on that day God settled from all the labor that He had created for the very purpose of its doing.]

Join in, gentlefolk, dear masters, my teachers:

You are blessed, Lord God-of-Us, King of the Cosmos, Maker of the fruit of the vine.

You are blessed, Lord God-of-Us, King of the Cosmos, who selected us from among every nation, and raised us above every culture, and sanctified us with His mitzvot. And it is with love—Lord God-of-Us—that You gave us [Shabbatot to rest and] holidays for our happiness, that you gave us festivals and seasons to rejoice, that you gave us the day [of this Shabbat and the day] of this Festival of Matzot in the season of our emancipation, and designated it [with love] as holy—a commemoration of the Exodus from Egypt. Because it was us that You elected, and us that You set apart from all other nations, and it was [the Shabbat and] the holidays sanctified by You [with love and with desire] with happiness and rejoicing that You bequeathed us. You are blessed, Lord, who sanctifies [the Shabbat and] Israel and the seasons.

622 BCE

During the reforms of
King Josiah, a "book
of instruction,"
most likely the core
of Deuteronomy, is
read to the public,
calling upon the
people of Israel to
offer a sacrifice to
God on Passover
(2 Kings: 22-23).

587 BCE

Jerusalem is conquered and destroyed by the army of Babylon, and the Israelites are taken captive as slaves. They live in forced exile for almost 50 years, until King Cyrus the Great permits them to return home in 538.

On Saturday night only, recite:

You are blessed, Lord God-of-Us, King of the Cosmos, Maker who bestows luminescence to the flame.

בָּרוּךְ אַתָּה יהוה, אֱלֹהֵינוּ מֶלֶךְ הָעוֹלָם, בּוֹרֵא מְאוֹרֵי הָאֵשׁ.

On Saturday night only, continue:

You are blessed, Lord God-of-Us, King of the Cosmos, who differentiates between the sanctified and the mundane, between light and dark, between Israel and the nations, between the seventh day and the six days of the Making. You differentiated between the holiness of Shabbat and the holy of the holiday, and you made the seventh day sacred above the six days of the Making. You held up and hallowed Your nation, Your Israel, in Your sanctity. You are blessed, Lord, the one who distinguishes between holy and holy.

בָּרוּךְ אַתָּה יהוה, אֱלֹהֵינוּ מֶלֶךְ הָעוֹלָם, הַמַּבְדִּיל בֵּין קֹדֶשׁ לְחוֹל, בֵּין אוֹר לְחֹשֶׁךְ, בֵּין יִשְׂרָאֵל לָעַמִּים, בֵּין יוֹם הַשְּׁבִיעִי לְשֵׁשֶׁת יְמֵי הַמַּעֲשֶׂה. בֵּין קְדֻשַּׁת שַׁבָּת לִקְדֻשַּׁת יוֹם טוֹב הִבְדַּלְתָּ, וְאֶת יוֹם הַשְּׁבִיעִי מִשֵּׁשֶׁת יְמֵי הַמַּעֲשֶׂה קִדַּשְׁתָּ, הִבְדַּלְתָּ וְקִדַּשְׁתָּ אֶת עַמְּךָ יִשְׂרָאֵל בִּקְדֻשָּׁתֶךָ. בָּרוּךְ אַתָּה יהוה, הַמַּבְדִּיל בֵּין קֹדֶשׁ לְקֹדֶשׁ.

On all nights, continue with the following blessing. Those who recited it during candle lighting, do not recite it now:

You are blessed, Lord God-of-Us, King of the Cosmos, who breathed life, and sustained life, and shepherded us through to the current season.

בָּרוּךְ אַתָּה יהוה, אֱלֹהֵינוּ מֶלֶךְ הָעוֹלָם, שֶׁהֶחֱיָנוּ וְקִיְּמָנוּ וְהִגִּיעָנוּ לַזְּמַן הַזֶּה.

While reclining to the left, drink at least most of the cup of wine.

The Passover seder is conducted in an orderly fashion, with each ritual performed at a certain time, in a certain way, according to thousands of years of tradition. This is surprising, as the Jewish people do not have a history of being particularly well organized. Even God Himself often seems engaged in convolution, a phrase which here means "as if He has not quite followed His own plan." If you look around your Passover table now, you will most certainly see the muddle and the mess of the world. There is likely a stain someplace on the tablecloth, or perhaps one of the glasses has a smudge. Soon things will be spilled. You might be sitting with people you do not know very well, or do not like very much, so your own emotional state is somewhat disordered. Nobody likes everything served at the Passover dinner, so there will be chaos within people's palates, and the room is likely to be either too cold or too hot for someone, creating a chaos of discomfort. Perhaps there is someone who has not yet been seated, even as the seder is beginning, because they are "checking on the food," a phrase which here means "sneaking a few bites" when they're supposed to be participating in the ceremony.

This is as it should be. Passover celebrates freedom, and while the evening will proceed in a certain order, it is the muddle and the mess around the order that represent the freedom that everyone deserves, and that far too many people have been denied. With that in mind, why not excuse yourself, in an orderly fashion at some point in the ceremony, so that you might check on the food?

Playground

"And you shall be to me a kingdom of priests and a holy nation." Exodus 19:6

On this night that is different from all other nights, it is fitting that we begin by recalling our own difference. But how are we Jews different from all other peoples?

We are chosen, the Haggadah tells us.

Unlike salvation, chosenness is a question, not an answer; the beginning of a journey, not its end. It will not take place in the future and, therefore, we do not hope or pray for it. Instead, like the Exodus from Egypt, being chosen is something that has happened to us already, something that we must remember and, in so doing, make present in every generation. As modern people, we are used to choosing; being chosen is much more difficult, at least for many of us. Some of us do not accept it at all.

In the book of Numbers, Balaam declares of Israel: "As I see them from the mountaintops, gaze on them from the heights, there is a people that dwells apart, not reckoned among the nations." Chosenness can sometimes feel like loneliness; a burden. Perhaps for this reason, the Haggadah reminds us that our chosenness is an expression of God's love and a source for rejoicing.

We might even say that wrestling with being chosen, like Jacob wrestling with God—or was it with himself?—is Jewishness itself. We might, like Rabbi Hillel, say that the rest is commentary. Yet this, after all, is a night for commentary; a night for asking questions that we have been chosen to ask.

House of Study

Time rushes on, impassive and unmarked. It's we who domesticate the flux, parceling it out into countable units so that we can situate ourselves within it: I am young and live in expectation, I am old and nearing the end of my days. Differentiation creates order, creates duration, creates the sense of our lives.

A religious calendar imposes further divisions on time, separating out hours to be regarded as so significant as to achieve holiness. That, after all, is the meaning of the Sabbath and holidays, the holy days. In the traditional Jewish calendar, the borders around the sacred hours are delineated with obsessive precision, the time of the onset of a holy day calculated to the last minute. The notion of the chosen is applied to temporality itself, and hours are carved out of the flux to gesture toward eternity.

The celebration of Passover emphasizes the imposition of an ordered structure over the formlessness of time. From the beginning to the end of the seder there is a multiplicity of stages, with procedural instructions overlaid all along the way. First you must do this, we are told, and now you must do that. Differentiation creates order, creates the sense of significance that makes duration endurable. And if there is a way toward sanctification in all of this, if such an ideal is even possible, then it lies somewhere here in the divisions, parting time as Moses parted the sea, effecting a separation where the extraordinary can make itself felt.

Library

Judaism, particularly in its American expression, is not thought of as a law-and-order religion. But it very much is, if not in the string-'em-up sense of the term—punishment in Judaism is accompanied by the promise of mercy. We are, of course, a people of laws, and we are also a people of order, of seder. Our foundation story, in the book of Genesis, is a tightly organized account of the making of order out of chaos. In the creation stories of other ancient peoples, we see gods who are in competition with man. This can make for narratives that are morally ambiguous and disorderly. In Judaism, there is no such ambiguity, and no such disorder; God orders the world through law.

In Judaism, law is holy. But not all laws. The laws of man must be subjected to a vigorous test: whether or not they conform to moral law as set forth by God. Martin Luther King Jr. wrote from the Birmingham city jail that "an unjust law is a human law that is not rooted in eternal law and natural law. Any law that uplifts human personality is just." King was arguing against laws that separated the races, and he turned to a leading thinker of his century to buttress the case: "Segregation, to use the terminology of the Jewish philosopher Martin Buber, substitutes an 'I-it' relationship for an 'I-Thou' relationship and ends up relegating persons to the status of things."

It is possible to imagine that King had in mind the story of Shifra and Puah, the midwives who delivered Moses, when he argued for the equality of all God's children. Passover is the most politically radical of all holidays in part because, as the scholar Nahum Sarna has noted, the book of Exodus contains the first known example in ancient literature of civil disobedience. Shifra and Puah were instructed by Pharaoh to kill the sons of the Israelites. Pharaoh was the law. But the law was unjust. So these two heroic midwives broke one law, and most certainly risked their lives, in order to honor a higher law: "The midwives feared God and they did not do as the king of Egypt spoke to them, and they allowed the boys to live." Without Shifra and Puah, no Moses; no liberation, no Sinai, no Torah. Their bravery forces us to ask ourselves: Are there times when we should have resisted an unjust man-made law, and did not?

Nation

Wash your hands, without reciting the usual blessing, and dry them. Remain silent until after karpas.

Urhatz

וּרְחַץ

Dip a small piece of vegetable in salt water and recite the blessing (keep in mind that this blessing also applies to the maror that will be eaten later):

Karpas

כַּרְפַּס

You are blessed, Lord God-of-Us, King of the Cosmos, who creates the earth's harvest.

בָּרוּךְ אַתָּה יהוה אֱלֹהֵינוּ מֶלֶךְ הָעוֹלָם,
בּוֹרֵא פְּרִי הָאֲדָמָה.

516 BCE

After the exiles'
return from Babylon,
the new temple
is dedicated on
Passover.

Yahatz

יַחַץ

Break the middle matzah into two. Wrap the larger part—the afikoman—and hide it from the children for later. (Before hiding the afikoman, some put it on their shoulders for a moment, to reenact the Israelites' posture when fleeing Egypt.) Return the smaller piece to between the two whole matzot.

500 BCE

The world's Jewish population is approximately 300,000, or about 0.2% of the total global population.

Magid מַגִּיד

The high priest of
Jerusalem responds
to a query from Jews
on the Nile island of
Elephantine on how
to properly observe
Passover: "In the
month of Nisan, let
there be a Passover.
...Do not work on
the 15th day and on
the 21st day. Also,
drink no intoxicants,
and anything in
which there is
leaven." Tonight,
the document is
in the Bildarchiv
Preussischer
Kulturbesitz in Berlin.

הָא לַחְמָא עַנְיָא דִי אֲכָלוּ אַבְהָתָנָא בְּאַרְעָא
דְמִצְרָיִם. כָּל דִכְפִין יֵיתֵי וְיֵיכֹל, כָּל דִצְרִיךְ יֵיתֵי וְיִפְסַח.
הָשַׁתָּא הָכָא, לְשָׁנָה הַבָּאָה בְּאַרְעָא דְיִשְׂרָאֵל.
הָשַׁתָּא עַבְדֵי, לְשָׁנָה הַבָּאָה בְּנֵי חוֹרִין.

יְהִי רָצוֹן מִלְפָנֶיךָ יהוה אֱלֹהֵינוּ וֵאלֹהֵי אֲבוֹתֵינוּ שֶׁכְּמוֹ שֶׁלָּקַחְתָּ גּוֹי מִקֶּרֶב גּוֹי וְהֶעֱבַרְתָּ
אֶת עַמְּךָ יִשְׂרָאֵל בְּתוֹךְ הַיָּם, כֵּן תְּרַחֵם עַל אַחֵינוּ כָּל בֵּית יִשְׂרָאֵל הַנְּתוּנִים
בְּצָרָה וּבְשִׁבְיָה, הָעוֹמְדִים בֵּין בַּיָּם וּבֵין בַּיַּבָּשָׁה. תַּצִילֵם וְתוֹצִיאֵם
מִצָּרָה לִרְוָחָה וּמֵאֲפֵלָה לְאוֹרָה וּמִשִּׁעְבּוּד לִגְאֻלָּה,
בִּמְהֵרָה בְיָמֵינוּ וְנֹאמַר אָמֵן.

Uncover the matzot and say:

This is the poor man's bread that our fathers ate in the land of Egypt. All who are bent with hunger, come and eat; all who are in dire straits, come share Passover with us. This year we are here, next year in the land of Israel. This year we are slaves, next year the liberated ones.

Just as You lifted nation from the belly of nation, and piloted Your people through the deep, may it be desirous before You, Lord God-of-Us and God of our fathers, to show compassion for our brothers, the whole house of Israel, to those hemmed in by misery and captivity and those trapped between sand and sea. Rescue and recover them—delivering them from gorge to meadow, from darkness to light. Break them free of their shackles and lead them on to salvation. Do it with speed and in our days, and let us all say, Amen.

Cover the matzot and move them to the side. Refill the cup.

"This year we are slaves," the Haggadah declares,

an odd presumption for it to make, as well as an anachronism. Slaves were what we were, not are, so what is the Haggadah talking about?

The open invitation that immediately precedes the baffling declaration suggests in what sense we still lack our freedom, as well as what we must do in order to possess what we do not possess and become what we still are not: "All who are bent with hunger, come and eat; all who are in dire straits, come share Passover with us." The needs of those outside our homes seem too distant to disturb us, and this is our impoverishment. Our failures in charity are chained to a narrowed vision of the world that makes too much of the differences between us, and this is our enslavement.

"All who are bent with hunger, come and eat."

This is one of those strange locutions linguists call a performative. The uttering of it itself constitutes an act. So, for example, one's saying, under the right circumstances, "I thee do wed" doesn't describe the action: it is the action. And so it is with this invitation to the needy. We utter these words, in true earnestness, and the utterance becomes an act of charity.

Words are so mysterious to us that word power can seem like magic power, which is why there are prayers, incantations, and curses. "Abracadabra" comes from the ancient Hebrew for "I will create with words." We do things with words. We confess and entreat. We threaten, wound, seduce, and forgive. And we perform acts of charity, as in this passage, where just such an act is deemed the means to end our slavery.

"Ha-Lahmah Anya" moves swiftly. It begins by describing the unleavened bread in terms of the remembered afflictions of our ancestors, then passes to the performance of a good deed, and finally ends by foreseeing our freedom. Past, present, and future are represented by words that first mourn, then perform, and then long—all of these embodying acts which are quintessentially Jewish.

Library

It is altogether proper that matzah is called the bread of affliction, because it has been afflicted more than any other foodstuff on earth. It is born in a searing-hot oven and then completely ignored for fifty-one weeks of the year while people walk around shamelessly eating leavened bread and

crackers. Then, Passover rolls around, and it is smeared with various substances, ground up into balls, and, in the morning, fried up into a counterfeit version of French toast. Everyone eats it and nobody likes it, and there's always one last box that sits untouched in a cupboard for months afterward, lonely, broken, and utterly unloved.

Of course it is practically impossible for free and fortunate people such as ourselves to envision a life of slavery, but as an exercise in imagining our ancestors, place a large square of matzah in your mouth and eat it. Listen to the cacophonous crunches in your ears like the blows of the slavedriver's whip. Feel the searing dryness in your mouth like the thirst of the Hebrew slaves for freedom. And then, with your mouth full of matzah, try to say the Shema, and watch the particles of oppression scatter across the table. Slavery spreads like a spray of crumbs, and it is very difficult to rid ourselves of slavery's great moral shame, which is why, even thousands of years after the Exodus, there are so many people enslaved, and why, even weeks after Passover, there are so many matzah crumbs in the house.

Playground

Poor Man's Bread

The rabbis teach us that in order to have Torah, we must first have bread; in order to sustain our souls, we must first sustain our bodies. But what is bread? And how much bread is enough?

House of Study

The answer to these questions can be found in the Torah itself. For there, we learn that when the Israelites were fleeing Egypt, when there was no time to spare, God commanded them to make the unleavened bread that we now raise before us, saying "This is the bread of affliction that our ancestors ate in the land of Egypt; let all those that are hungry enter and eat thereof."

Matzah is bread but just barely. Anything less would be mere flour and water; anything more would become the leavened bread that we eat during the rest of the year. Jewish tradition holds that no more than eighteen minutes may pass from the time we combine the flour and water to the time that we bake the mixture. Eighteen, of course, is the numerical value of the Hebrew word for "life." And so, matzah is both literally and symbolically the absolute minimum that we require for sustaining life and, therefore, the minimum that we require for Torah—the life of the soul.

Just as our ancestors only needed the "bread of the poor"—another meaning of ha-lahmah anya—as they made their way out of Egypt to receive the Torah, so too should we ask ourselves how much bread is enough and how much is too much to make an honest and soulful life possible today.

Nation

If there is a moment in the seder that should leave us feeling self-conscious, it is now. "This is the bread of affliction," we read. True enough; matzah is the quintessential discomfort food. But what follows is a problem: "All who are bent with hunger, come and eat." What's the problem, exactly? Judaism, after all, is not opposed to feeding the hungry (Jews even excel at feeding those who are already full). In fact, feeding the hungry is in some ways the mother of all mitzvot. And precisely because it is the most fundamental form of charity, this invitation to the hungry seems empty and hypocritical. Why? Because it comes too late. By the time we read this passage, we are seated, our hands are washed, the wine is poured, the table is crowded with fine dishes. And only now we invite the poor to join us?

Maybe this passage should be read a week, or a month, before Passover, when there would still be time to issue a meaningful invitation to a hungry person. But there is no provision in Judaism for such a pre-seder seder—and tampering with the seder would mean negating the very idea of seder. So we are left with an uncomfortable question: Is the Haggadah being cruel? Or merely disingenuous? How, as we fill our bellies with brisket, can we mourn the existence of hunger in the world and not feel like hypocrites? The Haggadah, of course, might be making a point at our expense. Could it be teaching us that this night, in one crucial way, is just like all other nights? On all other nights we eat to satisfaction without a thought for the hungry stranger. Tonight, we speak of hunger, but do nothing to alleviate it. In Judaism, it is not the thought that counts, but the deed. Is the Haggadah telling us to get up right now from this table and find a hungry person to feed?

Circa 200 BCE

Circa 300 BCE

The Greek Sibylline oracle writes of the Jews: "Every land is full of you, and every sea...it is thy fate to leave thine holy soil."

The Samaritan religion splits from mainstream Judaism to practice its own form of monotheism, centered on Mount Gezerim rather than the Temple in Jerusalem.

מַה נִּשְׁתַּנָּה הַלַּיְלָה הַזֶּה מִכָּל הַלֵּילוֹת?

שֶׁבְּכָל הַלֵּילוֹת אָנוּ אוֹכְלִין חָמֵץ וּמַצָּה,

הַלַּיְלָה הַזֶּה - **כֻּלּוֹ מַצָּה.**

שֶׁבְּכָל הַלֵּילוֹת אָנוּ אוֹכְלִין שְׁאָר יְרָקוֹת,

הַלַּיְלָה הַזֶּה **מָרוֹר.**

שֶׁבְּכָל הַלֵּילוֹת אֵין אָנוּ מַטְבִּילִין אֲפִילוּ פַּעַם אֶחָת,

הַלַּיְלָה הַזֶּה שְׁתֵּי פְּעָמִים.

שֶׁבְּכָל הַלֵּילוֹת אָנוּ אוֹכְלִין בֵּין יוֹשְׁבִין וּבֵין מְסֻבִּין,

הַלַּיְלָה הַזֶּה כֻּלָּנוּ מְסֻבִּין.

The following four questions are asked by a child, or the youngest able participant.

What makes this night different
from all other nights?

On all other nights we eat hametz and matzah,
on this night, we eat only matzah.

On all other nights we eat vegetables of all types,
on this night, we eat maror.

On all other nights we don't dip—not even once,
on this night, we dip twice.

On all other nights we eat either sitting up or leaning back,
on this night, everyone leans.

עֲבָדִים הָיִינוּ לְפַרְעֹה בְּמִצְרָיִם,

וַיּוֹצִיאֵנוּ יְהוָה אֱלֹהֵינוּ מִשָּׁם בְּיָד חֲזָקָה וּבִזְרוֹעַ נְטוּיָה.

וְאִלּוּ לֹא הוֹצִיא הַקָּדוֹשׁ בָּרוּךְ הוּא אֶת אֲבוֹתֵינוּ מִמִּצְרַיִם,

הֲרֵי אָנוּ וּבָנֵינוּ וּבְנֵי בָנֵינוּ מְשֻׁעְבָּדִים הָיִינוּ לְפַרְעֹה בְּמִצְרָיִם.

וַאֲפִילוּ כֻּלָּנוּ חֲכָמִים, כֻּלָּנוּ נְבוֹנִים, כֻּלָּנוּ זְקֵנִים, כֻּלָּנוּ

יוֹדְעִים אֶת הַתּוֹרָה, מִצְוָה עָלֵינוּ לְסַפֵּר בִּיצִיאַת מִצְרָיִם.

וְכָל הַמַּרְבֶּה לְסַפֵּר בִּיצִיאַת מִצְרַיִם

הֲרֵי זֶה מְשֻׁבָּח.

Return the matzot to their place. Uncover them and say:

Slaves is what we were—slaves to Pharaoh in Egypt. And wrested free, were we, by the Lord God-of-Us, lifted out of that place in the mighty hand of an outstretched arm. And if the Holy One, blessed is He, had not taken our fathers out of Egypt, then what of us? We, and our children, and our children's children, would be enslaved to Pharaoh in Egypt. Were it that we were all learned and all enlightened, all of us rich with the wisdom of old age and well versed in the Torah, *still* the obligation to tell of the Exodus from Egypt would rest upon us. All who are expansive in their telling of the Exodus from Egypt are worthy of praise.

The Year 0

The world's Jewish
population is
approximately
5 million, and
represents an
all-time high of 2%
of the total global
population.

33 CE

Jesus of Nazareth
celebrates Passover
with a seder that
will be known to
Christians as the
Last Supper.

In late summer, on Tisha b'Av, or the ninth day of the Hebrew month of Av, Roman forces commanded by Titus conquer Jerusalem and destroy the Temple.

מַעֲשֶׂה בְּרַבִּי אֱלִיעֶזֶר וְרַבִּי יְהוֹשֻׁעַ וְרַבִּי אֶלְעָזָר בֶּן
עֲזַרְיָה וְרַבִּי עֲקִיבָא וְרַבִּי טַרְפוֹן, שֶׁהָיוּ מְסֻבִּין בִּבְנֵי בְרַק, וְהָיוּ
מְסַפְּרִים בִּיצִיאַת מִצְרַיִם כָּל אוֹתוֹ הַלַּיְלָה, עַד שֶׁבָּאוּ תַלְמִידֵיהֶם
וְאָמְרוּ לָהֶם: רַבּוֹתֵינוּ, הִגִּיעַ זְמַן קְרִיאַת שְׁמַע שֶׁל שַׁחֲרִית.

אָמַר רַבִּי אֶלְעָזָר בֶּן עֲזַרְיָה: הֲרֵי אֲנִי כְּבֶן שִׁבְעִים שָׁנָה, וְלֹא
זָכִיתִי שֶׁתֵּאָמֵר יְצִיאַת מִצְרַיִם בַּלֵּילוֹת, עַד שֶׁדְּרָשָׁהּ בֶּן זוֹמָא,
שֶׁנֶּאֱמַר: לְמַעַן תִּזְכֹּר אֶת יוֹם צֵאתְךָ מֵאֶרֶץ
מִצְרַיִם כָּל יְמֵי חַיֶּיךָ. יְמֵי חַיֶּיךָ - הַיָּמִים. כָּל יְמֵי חַיֶּיךָ -
הַלֵּילוֹת. וַחֲכָמִים אוֹמְרִים: יְמֵי חַיֶּיךָ - הָעוֹלָם הַזֶּה. כָּל יְמֵי
חַיֶּיךָ - לְהָבִיא לִימוֹת הַמָּשִׁיחַ.

On Passover, after many months under siege, the last remnants of the rebellion against Rome commit collective suicide in the desert fortress of Masada. After the founding of the State of Israel in 1948, the site becomes one of the country's most popular tourist attractions. Soldiers in the Israeli army are initiated with a pledge from a 1927 poem by the Russian émigré Yitzhak Lamdan—"Masada shall not fall again."

There was an incident with Rabbi Eliezer and Rabbi Yehoshua and Rabbi Elazar son of Azaria and Rabbi Akiva and Rabbi Tarfon. They were gathered in Bnei Brak and recounting the Exodus from Egypt all through the night, right up until their disciples came and said to them: Dear Rabbis, the time for the recitation of the dawn Shema has arrived.

Rabbi Elazar son of Azaria said: Here, I might as well be seventy years old, and still, I could not persuade others to tell the tale of Exodus during the nights, not until ben-Zoma illuminated it this way: As it is written, *So that you remember the day of your exit from Egypt all the days of your life.*

The days of your life—the days; *all the days of your life*—the nights as well.

And the sages say: *The days of your life*—this world; *all the days of your life*—the tale be told even after the coming of the Messiah.

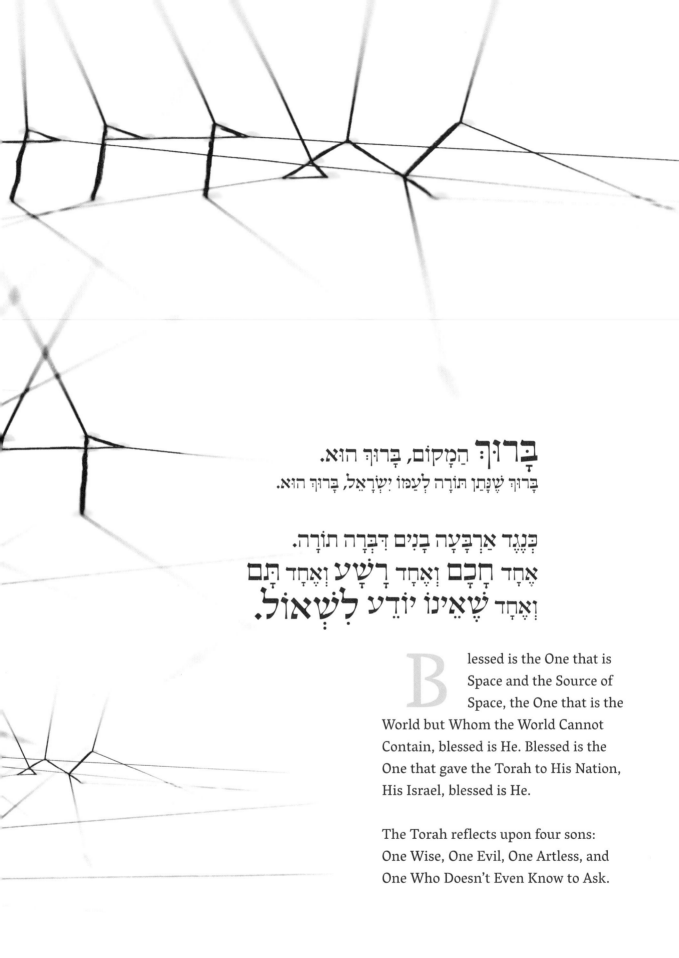

בָּרוּךְ הַמָּקוֹם, בָּרוּךְ הוּא.
בָּרוּךְ שֶׁנָּתַן תּוֹרָה לְעַמּוֹ יִשְׂרָאֵל, בָּרוּךְ הוּא.

כְּנֶגֶד אַרְבָּעָה בָנִים דִּבְּרָה תוֹרָה.
אֶחָד חָכָם וְאֶחָד רָשָׁע וְאֶחָד תָּם
וְאֶחָד שֶׁאֵינוֹ יוֹדֵעַ לִשְׁאוֹל.

B lessed is the One that is Space and the Source of Space, the One that is the World but Whom the World Cannot Contain, blessed is He. Blessed is the One that gave the Torah to His Nation, His Israel, blessed is He.

The Torah reflects upon four sons: One Wise, One Evil, One Artless, and One Who Doesn't Even Know to Ask.

Circa 75

In his history of
the ancient world,
the Jewish scholar
Josephus Flavius
recounts the life of
Moses, including the
highly unlikely claim
that after crossing
the Red Sea, Moses
composed a hymn
of praise to God in
Greek hexameter.
Now, he writes, the
Jews "are scattered
in all the towns,
and it is difficult
to find a place in
all the inhabited
world which has not
received them."

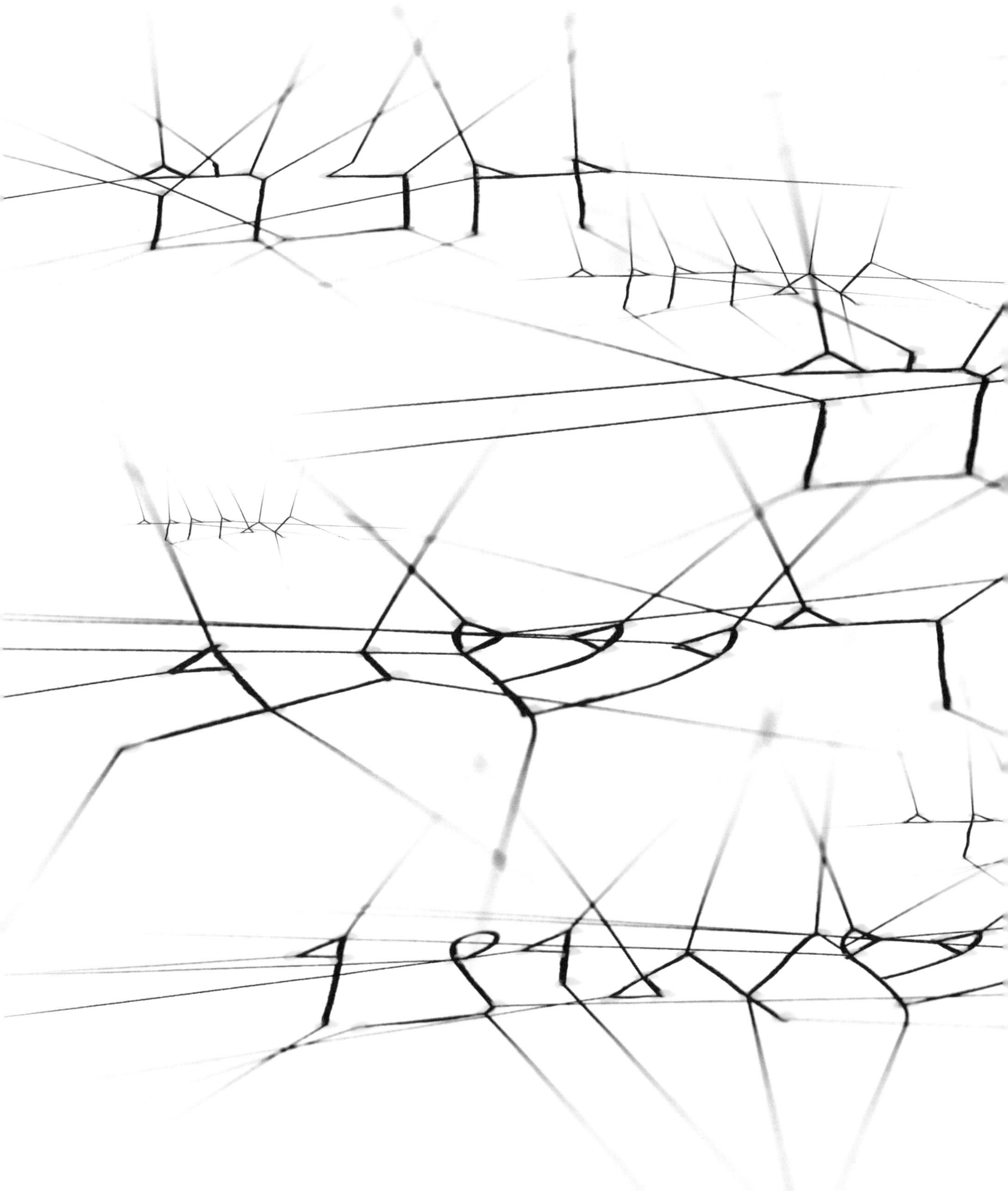

חָכָם מַה הוּא אוֹמֵר? מָה הָעֵדֹת וְהַחֻקִּים וְהַמִּשְׁפָּטִים אֲשֶׁר צִוָּה יהוה אֱלֹהֵינוּ אוֹתָנוּ? וְאַף אַתָּה אֱמָר לֹו כְּהִלְכוֹת הַפֶּסַח עַד: אֵין מַפְטִירִין אַחַר הַפֶּסַח אֲפִיקוֹמָן.

רָשָׁע מַה הוּא אוֹמֵר? מָה הָעֲבוֹדָה הַזֹּאת לָכֶם? לָכֶם וְלֹא לֹו. וּלְפִי שֶׁהוֹצִיא אֶת עַצְמוֹ מִן הַכְּלָל כָּפַר בָּעִקָּר. וְאַף אַתָּה הַקְהֵה אֶת שִׁנָּיו וֶאֱמָר לֹו: בַּעֲבוּר זֶה עָשָׂה יהוה לִי בְּצֵאתִי מִמִּצְרָיִם. לִי וְלֹא לֹו. אִלּוּ הָיָה שָׁם, לֹא הָיָה נִגְאָל.

תָּם מַה הוּא אוֹמֵר? מַה זֹּאת? וְאָמַרְתָּ אֵלָיו: בְּחֹזֶק יָד הוֹצִיאָנוּ יהוה מִמִּצְרַיִם מִבֵּית עֲבָדִים.

וְשֶׁאֵינוֹ יוֹדֵעַ לִשְׁאוֹל, אַתְּ פְּתַח לֹו, שֶׁנֶּאֱמַר: וְהִגַּדְתָּ לְבִנְךָ בַּיּוֹם הַהוּא לֵאמֹר, בַּעֲבוּר זֶה עָשָׂה יהוה לִי בְּצֵאתִי מִמִּצְרָיִם.

יָכוֹל מֵרֹאשׁ חֹדֶשׁ, תַּלְמוּד לוֹמַר בַּיּוֹם הַהוּא. אִי בַּיּוֹם הַהוּא, יָכוֹל מִבְּעוֹד יוֹם, תַּלְמוּד לוֹמַר בַּעֲבוּר זֶה. בַּעֲבוּר זֶה לֹא אָמַרְתִּי אֶלָּא בְּשָׁעָה שֶׁיֵּשׁ מַצָּה וּמָרוֹר מֻנָּחִים לְפָנֶיךָ.

Reeling from the destruction of the Second Temple, the scholars of the Palestinian city of Yavneh canonize the ritual of the seder. Since the traditional Passover sacrifice in Jerusalem is no longer possible, they devise this portable way to commemorate and celebrate the Exodus with a festive meal. Instead of the temple sacrifice, the communal meal with its symbolic lamb shank is now the focus of the holiday. No matter where they dwell, Jews in the Diaspora will tell the story of the Exodus together over the meal. Tonight, we will tell it once again.

The Wise One, what does he say? *"What are the testimonies, the laws and judgments, that the Lord God-of-Us commanded you follow?"* It falls upon you to guide him through all the obligations of Pesach, including: It is forbidden to eat anything after the Passover meal.

The Evil One, what does he say? *"What does this type of worship mean to you?"* To you and not to him. And by divorcing himself from the community, he denies our very essence. Moreover, you must blunt the bite of his words, by telling him: *"For this purpose the Lord labored on my behalf by taking me out of Egypt."* For me and not for him. Had he been there, he would stand undelivered.

The Artless One, what does he say? *"What is this?"* And say to him: *"With the strength of a mighty hand we were delivered from Egypt, the house of servitude."*

And the One Who Doesn't Even Know to Ask, you should open up the story for him, as it is said: *"And on that day, tell your son, saying, For this purpose, the Lord labored on my behalf by taking me out of Egypt."*

One might think the recounting should begin at the start of the month. But there is a verse that tells us, *on that day.* If it is on that day, one might then think, while it is yet day. But that same verse tells us, *for this purpose.* For this purpose the story is not recounted except during the hour when there is matzah and maror spread out before you.

"And he [Moses] took the book of the covenant and read it in the hearing of the people; and they said: 'All that the Lord has spoken, we will do and we will hear.'" Exodus 24:7

Tonight we celebrate the liberation of our ancestors from slavery in Egypt. But does liberation mean freedom? Of course, we say. After all, the Haggadah itself declares: "He took us from slavery to freedom, from mourning to festivity, and from deep darkness to great light and from bondage to redemption." But nothing is simple in Torah.

According to the book of Exodus, when the Torah was given at Sinai, the Israelites accepted its commandments without first hearing what they would be. Thus they declared: Naaseh ve-nishmah, "We will do and we will hear." But even the simple son of the Haggadah asks, "What is this?" when presented with the story of the Exodus.

House of Study

Were the Israelites at Sinai so naïve that they were like the son who does not even know how to ask? Or did they knowingly decide to take a leap of faith and exchange the yoke of slavery in Egypt for what the rabbis call "the yoke of heaven"—no questions asked? And in so doing, did they give up the freedom that they had just acquired in leaving Egypt?

The wicked son of the Haggadah believes in freedom, and so many of us are drawn to him. Freedom, for the wicked son, means denying that the laws of the Torah affirmed by the wise son apply to him. But that is not all. The wicked son also denies that he is a member of the Jewish community, what the rabbis call klal yisrael. By asserting his individual freedom, the Haggadah declares, the wicked son has exempted himself from the liberation from Egypt: "If he had been there, he would not have been redeemed."

Here, it appears, we have freedom without liberation. But does this also mean that the Torah believes in liberation without freedom?

Some scholars believe there are four kinds of parents as well. The Wise Parent is an utter bore.

"Listen closely, because you are younger than I am," says the Wise Parent, "and I will go on and on about Jewish history, based on some foggy memories of my own religious upbringing, as well as an article in a Jewish journal I have recently skimmed." The Wise Parent must be faced with a small smile of dim interest.

The Wicked Parent tries to cram the story of our liberation into a set of narrow opinions about the world. "The Lord led us out of Egypt," the Wicked Parent says, "which is why I support a bloodthirsty foreign policy and am tired of certain types of people causing problems." The Wicked Parent should be told in a firm voice, "With a strong hand God rescued the Jews from bondage, but it was my own clumsy hand that spilled hot soup in your lap."

The Simple Parent does not grasp the concept of freedom. "There will be no macaroons until you eat all of your brisket," says the Simple Parent, at a dinner honoring the liberation of oppressed peoples. "Also, stop slouching at the table." In answer to such statements, the Wise Child will roll his eyes in the direction of the ceiling and declare, "Let my people go!" The Parent Who Is Unable to Inquire has had too much wine, and should be excused from the table.

Playground

Four Sons

Questions, even the most irreverent, seed the freedom that we celebrate tonight.

When God, taking Abraham into his confidence, announced the intended destruction of those sinful cities of the plain, S'dom and Gemorrah, the man responded with rebellion. "Heaven forbid for you to do a thing like this, to deal death to the innocent along with the guilty. Heaven forbid for you! The judge of all the earth—will he not do what is just?"

The irreverence displayed here takes the breath away. But even more breathtaking is the divine response. God doesn't consume his inquisitor in a pillar of fire. Instead the proverbial Grounding of Moral Truth submits himself to Abraham's questioning. And had he not, had he instead flamed up in his aggrieved purity, then the story we tell tonight could never have been written, not a word of it.

Abraham's passion for questions has been bequeathed to many of his seed, including the philosopher Baruch Spinoza, who was banished from his community for asking the wrong questions. He changed his name from the Hebrew Baruch to the Latin Benedictus, and went out into the world and made so great a difference in freeing minds from superstition that the world itself changed for the better, and the people who had disowned him have lived to flourish thanks to those changes.

There is a son who sits at the table, harboring an irreverent question, one that challenges the assumptions that have brought this family to this table for many generations. If the struggles with his question lead him away from the answers of his father, what then? Must lineage dictate the son's interpretation of the world? This, fundamentally, is this son's—or this daughter's—question, and the answer to it is by no means self-evident. Can a tradition that presents a God who suffered himself to be morally interrogated find no better answer than the label of wicked, either silencing the questioners into submission or banishing them forever from their seats at the table?

The wicked son is not wicked in any of the usual ways. He is not violent or sexually immoral; he does not keep

slaves or steal. His wickedness is that he is indifferent to the fate of the Jewish people. "What is this to you?" he asks. "To *you*," not "To *me*." What he is saying, in effect, is "The fate of my people is not my concern." Here is a vexing demand sometimes made of young Jews by their elders in America today: You should worry about Jews more than you worry about non-Jews. In the shtetls of the Pale, or the ghettos of Morocco, this was not such a difficult thing to ask, because who had a choice? Jews were sequestered from the world, so why should they have cared about its problems? But in America, this unique Diaspora nation, a place that comprehensively accepts, even embraces, its Jewish citizens, this becomes a more troubling proposition. Which is why a war rages in the souls of American Jews, the war between the universal and the particular. Is it not a form of chauvinism to declare that the fate of Ethiopian Jews is an overriding concern of the American Jewish community, but what happens to non-Jewish Ethiopians is only a marginal concern?

This question arises anew in each successive generation. Those Jews who were college students in the 1980s experienced this dilemma rather directly. Two liberation movements then preoccupied many campuses: the struggle against apartheid in South Africa, and the fight to free Soviet Jewry. Both were righteous causes. But one benefited Jews directly, and the other didn't. Many Jews made the struggle against white South Africa their cause. This was to their everlasting credit, as Jews and as moral beings. But what would have happened if no American Jew had made the cause of Soviet Jewry his own? Here is the same question put another way: Was it parochial or chauvinistic of the nations of sub-Saharan Africa to fight apartheid with singular focus?

There are so many challenges embedded in Judaism, but perhaps this is the greatest one of all: How do we balance our faith's demand to care especially for our fellow Jews, and care especially for the entire world, at the same time?

Mohammed, the founder and prophet of Islam, leaves Mecca for Medina, a center of Jewish cultural life. Rites of Judaism are modified and displaced by new Islamic ones influenced by Judaism, including a daily regimen of five prayers, laws of charity, fast days, and prohibitions against unclean food. The second caliph of Islam, Omar, bans Jews and adherents to other faiths from Arabia, but upon the Muslim conquest of Jerusalem in 638, the new rulers repeal the Christian ban on Jewish settlement.

מִתְּחִלָּה **עוֹבְדֵי עֲבוֹדָה זָרָה** הָיוּ אֲבוֹתֵינוּ, וְעַכְשָׁיו קֵרְבָנוּ הַמָּקוֹם לַעֲבוֹדָתוֹ, שֶׁנֶּאֱמַר: וַיֹּאמֶר יְהוֹשֻׁעַ אֶל כָּל הָעָם, כֹּה אָמַר יהוה אֱלֹהֵי יִשְׂרָאֵל: בְּעֵבֶר הַנָּהָר יָשְׁבוּ אֲבוֹתֵיכֶם מֵעוֹלָם, תֶּרַח אֲבִי אַבְרָהָם וַאֲבִי נָחוֹר. וַיַּעַבְדוּ אֱלֹהִים אֲחֵרִים. **וָאֶקַּח אֶת אֲבִיכֶם**, אֶת אַבְרָהָם, מֵעֵבֶר הַנָּהָר, וָאוֹלֵךְ אוֹתוֹ בְּכָל אֶרֶץ כְּנָעַן. וָאַרְבֶּה אֶת זַרְעוֹ, וָאֶתֶּן לוֹ אֶת יִצְחָק. וָאֶתֵּן לְיִצְחָק אֶת יַעֲקֹב וְאֶת עֵשָׂו. וָאֶתֵּן לְעֵשָׂו אֶת הַר שֵׂעִיר לָרֶשֶׁת אוֹתוֹ. וְיַעֲקֹב וּבָנָיו יָרְדוּ מִצְרָיִם.

וְיַעֲקֹב וּבָנָיו
יָרְדוּ מִצְרָיִם

At first our fathers were beholden to idols. Then the Omnipresent brought us close to His worship, as it is written: *And Joshua said to the whole of the nation, So says the Lord, God of Israel: Your fathers settled on the far side of the river forever ago—Terah, father of Abraham and father of Nahor—and they worshipped other Gods. And I took your father, took Abraham, from across that river, and I walked him through the whole land of Canaan. And I made plentiful his seed, and I gave him Isaac. And I gave Isaac, Jacob and Esau. And I gave Mount Seir to Esau as a legacy. And Jacob and his sons went down to Egypt.*

In a handwritten scrawl, an anonymous Palestinian Jew composes a Haggadah, now one of the oldest surviving versions on earth. The Haggadah finds its way into a Cairo synagogue's genizah, or repository for texts containing the name of God, and is excavated 2,477 years later by the prominent Anglo-American rabbi Solomon Schechter. Tonight, it is in the archives of the Jewish Theological Seminary in New York City.

בָּרוּךְ שׁוֹמֵר הַבְטָחָתוֹ לְיִשְׂרָאֵל, בָּרוּךְ הוּא.

שֶׁהַקָּדוֹשׁ בָּרוּךְ הוּא חִשֵּׁב אֶת הַקֵּץ לַעֲשׂוֹת כְּמָה שֶׁאָמַר לְאַבְרָהָם אָבִינוּ בִּבְרִית

בֵּין הַבְּתָרִים, שֶׁנֶּאֱמַר: וַיֹּאמֶר לְאַבְרָם, יָדֹעַ תֵּדַע כִּי גֵר יִהְיֶה זַרְעֲךָ בְּאֶרֶץ לֹא

לָהֶם, וַעֲבָדוּם וְעִנּוּ אֹתָם אַרְבַּע מֵאוֹת שָׁנָה, וְגַם אֶת הַגּוֹי אֲשֶׁר יַעֲבֹדוּ

דָן אָנֹכִי, וְאַחֲרֵי כֵן יֵצְאוּ בִּרְכֻשׁ גָּדוֹל.

B lessed is the One Who Preserves his pledges to Israel, blessed is He. For the Holy One, Blessed is He, envisioned the end of an era in order to do as he told our father Abraham in the Covenant of the Pieces; as it is written: *And He said to Abraham, Know and keep knowing that your offspring will be sojourners in a land that is not their land, and they will slave for their masters and be tortured by them for four hundred years. Know also that I will stand in judgment of their enslavers, and in the wake of that judgment your people will go out with great wealth.*

930

The Babylonian scholar Saadia Gaon sets the standard template for future Haggadot in his book on the order and arrangement of prayers.

וְהִיא שֶׁעָמְדָה לַאֲבוֹתֵינוּ וְלָנוּ, שֶׁלֹּא אֶחָד בִּלְבָד עָמַד עָלֵינוּ לְכַלּוֹתֵנוּ, אֶלָּא שֶׁבְּכָל דּוֹר וָדוֹר עוֹמְדִים עָלֵינוּ לְכַלּוֹתֵנוּ, וְהַקָּדוֹשׁ בָּרוּךְ הוּא מַצִּילֵנוּ מִיָּדָם.

1000

The world's Jewish
population is
approximately 1.3
million, or about
0.5% of the total
global population.

Circa 1000

As Jewish
communities
expand into Central
and Northern
Europe, they begin
to develop a new
vernacular language.
Like Judeo-Arabic,
Judeo-Farsi, and
Judeo-Spanish,
or Ladino, the
language of Yiddish
combines elements
of both Hebrew
and local tongues
to provide an
adaptable medium
of communication for
Jews. Over the next
millennium, Yiddish
evolves and expands
to become a lingua
franca for Jews from
the Netherlands to
the Balkans and the
Russian Empire.

*Cover the matzot.
Raise the cup
and say:*

And it was this that stood fast for our fathers and for us—
unwavering. For it was not one alone who stood over us,
a heel on our necks, bent on our annihilation, but, in
generation after generation, they rise up against us, intent on destroying
us. And yet, the Holy One, blessed is He, breaks their grip and we are saved.

*Place the cup back
down, uncover
the matzot, and
continue:*

*T*he Aramean disappeared my father, and he went down to Egypt, and lingered there with a small group. And it was there he transformed us into a great nation, massive and many. And they did us evil, those Egyptians, and they tortured us, saddling us with punishing work. And we cried out to the Lord, God of our fathers, and the Lord heard our voices, and He saw our torture and our toil, and the great pressure upon us. And the Lord lifted us out of Egypt in the mighty hand of an outstretched arm, with an awesome spectacle, with signs and undeniable wonders.

Based on the
harvest, the
Karaites—a Jewish
sect that accepts
only the Bible,
not the Mishna
or Talmud, as a
source of religious
authority—set a
different date for
Passover. As a result,
Karaites sometimes
celebrate Passover a
month earlier or later
than the rest of the
world's Jews.

אֲרַמִּי אֹבֵד אָבִי, וַיֵּרֶד מִצְרַיְמָה, וַיָּגָר שָׁם בִּמְתֵי מְעָט;
וַיְהִי שָׁם לְגוֹי גָּדוֹל, עָצוּם וָרָב.
וַיָּרֵעוּ אֹתָנוּ הַמִּצְרִים וַיְעַנּוּנוּ, וַיִּתְּנוּ עָלֵינוּ עֲבֹדָה קָשָׁה.
וַנִּצְעַק אֶל יהוה אֱלֹהֵי אֲבֹתֵינוּ; וַיִּשְׁמַע יהוה אֶת קֹלֵנוּ, וַיַּרְא אֶת עָנְיֵנוּ וְאֶת
עֲמָלֵנוּ וְאֶת לַחֲצֵנוּ. וַיּוֹצִאֵנוּ יהוה מִמִּצְרַיִם, בְּיָד חֲזָקָה
וּבִזְרֹעַ נְטוּיָה וּבְמֹרָא גָּדֹל, וּבְאֹתוֹת וּבְמֹפְתִים.

The scientist and
rabbinic sage
Moses ben Maimon,
also known as
Maimonedes, is
born in Cordoba.
After the Almohad
Muslim conquest of
Spain, the Maimon
family flees Cordoba
for Fez, Morocco,
in 1159. In 1165,
Maimonedes leaves
Fez for St. Jean d'Acre
(modern-day Akko),
making pilgrimages
to Hebron and
Jerusalem before
leaving for
Alexandria. He ends
his wanderings in
1166, when he settles
in Cairo, where he
remains until his
death in 1204.

צֵא וּלְמַד: מַה בִּקֵּשׁ לָבָן הָאֲרַמִּי לַעֲשׂוֹת
לְיַעֲקֹב אָבִינוּ, שֶׁפַּרְעֹה לֹא גָזַר אֶלָּא עַל
הַזְּכָרִים, וְלָבָן בִּקֵּשׁ לַעֲקוֹר אֶת הַכֹּל. שֶׁנֶּאֱמַר:
אֲרַמִּי אֹבֵד אָבִי וַיֵּרֶד מִצְרַיְמָה, וַיָּגָר שָׁם בִּמְתֵי מְעָט;
וַיְהִי שָׁם לְגוֹי גָּדוֹל, עָצוּם וָרָב.

Venture off and learn: What did Lavan the Aramean seek to do to Jacob our father? Something that Pharaoh decreed against the male offspring, but which Lavan sought in totality—to uproot them all. As it is written: *The Aramean disappeared my father, and he went down to Egypt, and lingered there with a small group. And it was there he transformed us into a great nation, massive and many.*

וַיֵּרֶד מִצְרַיְמָה. אָנוּס עַל פִּי הַדִּבּוּר, כְּמָה שֶׁנֶּאֱמַר: יָדֹעַ תֵּדַע כִּי גֵר יִהְיֶה זַרְעֲךָ בְּאֶרֶץ לֹא לָהֶם, וַעֲבָדוּם וְעִנּוּ אֹתָם אַרְבַּע מֵאוֹת שָׁנָה.

וַיָּגָר שָׁם. מְלַמֵּד שֶׁלֹּא יָרַד יַעֲקֹב אָבִינוּ לְהִשְׁתַּקֵּעַ בְּמִצְרַיִם אֶלָּא לָגוּר שָׁם, שֶׁנֶּאֱמַר: וַיֹּאמְרוּ אֶל פַּרְעֹה, לָגוּר בָּאָרֶץ בָּאנוּ, כִּי אֵין מִרְעֶה לַצֹּאן אֲשֶׁר לַעֲבָדֶיךָ, כִּי כָבֵד הָרָעָב בְּאֶרֶץ כְּנָעַן, וְעַתָּה יֵשְׁבוּ נָא עֲבָדֶיךָ בְּאֶרֶץ גֹּשֶׁן.

בִּמְתֵי מְעָט. כְּמָה שֶׁנֶּאֱמַר: בְּשִׁבְעִים נֶפֶשׁ יָרְדוּ אֲבֹתֶיךָ מִצְרַיְמָה וְעַתָּה שָׂמְךָ יהוה אֱלֹהֶיךָ כְּכוֹכְבֵי הַשָּׁמַיִם לָרֹב.

וַיְהִי שָׁם לְגוֹי גָּדוֹל. מְלַמֵּד שֶׁהָיוּ יִשְׂרָאֵל מְצֻיָּנִים שָׁם, מְסֻמָּנִים בְּמִצְוֹת כְּגוֹי בִּפְנֵי עַצְמוֹ; לֹא נֶחְשְׁדוּ עַל הָעֲרָיוֹת, וְלֹא עַל לְשׁוֹן הָרָע; וְלֹא שִׁנּוּ אֶת שְׁמָם וְלֹא שִׁנּוּ אֶת לְשׁוֹנָם.

עָצוּם וָרָב. כְּמָה שֶׁנֶּאֱמַר: וּבְנֵי יִשְׂרָאֵל פָּרוּ וַיִּשְׁרְצוּ וַיִּרְבּוּ וַיַּעַצְמוּ בִּמְאֹד מְאֹד, וַתִּמָּלֵא הָאָרֶץ אֹתָם.

וָרָב. כְּמָה שֶׁנֶּאֱמַר, רְבָבָה כְּצֶמַח הַשָּׂדֶה נְתַתִּיךְ, וַתִּרְבִּי וַתִּגְדְּלִי וַתָּבֹאִי בַּעֲדִי עֲדָיִים, שָׁדַיִם נָכֹנוּ וּשְׂעָרֵךְ צִמֵּחַ, וְאַתְּ עֵרֹם וְעֶרְיָה; וָאֶעֱבֹר עָלַיִךְ וָאֶרְאֵךְ מִתְבּוֹסֶסֶת בְּדָמָיִךְ, וָאֹמַר לָךְ, בְּדָמַיִךְ חֲיִי, וָאֹמַר לָךְ, בְּדָמַיִךְ חֲיִי.

1171

In the first ritual murder accusation in continental Europe, the Jews of Blois, France, are accused of crucifying a Christian child during Passover and throwing the corpse into the Loire. In retaliation, over 30 Jewish men and women are burned at the stake.

1159

The Spanish traveler and chronicler Benjamin of Tudela leaves Spain for Provence, sails to Marseille and Genoa, and makes his way south to Rome. He then sails to Corfu and Constantinople, the Aegean islands, the Syrian coast, Damascus, Baghdad, Palestine, and Egypt. In 1172, he finally returns home to Tudela.

*A*nd he went down to Egypt. Driven there by the Spoken Word. As it was said by Him: *Know, and keep knowing, that your offspring will be sojourners in a land that is not their land, and they will slave for their masters, and be tortured by them for four hundred years.*

And lingered there. This teaches us that Jacob our father didn't go down to settle in Egypt but to linger there, as it is written: *And they said to Pharaoh, We came to linger in this land, because absent is the grazing for the sheep of your servants, because heavy is the famine in the land of Canaan, and presently, prithee, let your servants encamp in the land of Goshen.*

With a small group. As it is written: *With seventy souls your fathers descended to Egypt, and now the Lord your God has set you as the stars in heaven, a multitude.*

And it was there He transformed us into a great nation. This teaches us, it was *there* that Israel became exceptional, distinguished through mitzvot—distinct as a nation unto itself. Neither suspected of unchastities, nor of noxious talk. And they did not pervert their names, and they did not pervert their language.

Massive and many. As it is written: *And the children of Israel were fruitful and fecund and teeming, and became massive in the extremity of the extreme. And the land was awash with them.*

And many. As it is written: *I made you teem like the wildflower. And I made you many. And I grew you, and you came back lavishly matured—your breasts consummate and your hair in bloom, and you were naked and bare; and I passed over you, and spied you steeped in your blood. And I said to you, "In your blood, live!" And I said to you, "In your blood, live!"*

Pilgrims to the monastery of Ferrara, Italy, claim that "they had seen a certain Jew in Armenia who had been present at the Passion of the Lord, and, as He was going to His martyrdom, drove Him along wickedly with...'Go, go thou temper and seducer, to receive what you have earned.' Jesus... answered him: 'I go, and you will await me until I come again.'" The tale becomes the first written account of the European legend of the Wandering Jew, condemned to roam the world without sanctuary until the Second Coming of Christ.

וַיָּרֵעוּ אֹתָנוּ הַמִּצְרִים וַיְעַנּוּנוּ, וַיִּתְּנוּ עָלֵינוּ עֲבֹדָה קָשָׁה.

A nd they did us evil, those Egyptians, and they tortured us, saddling us with punishing work.

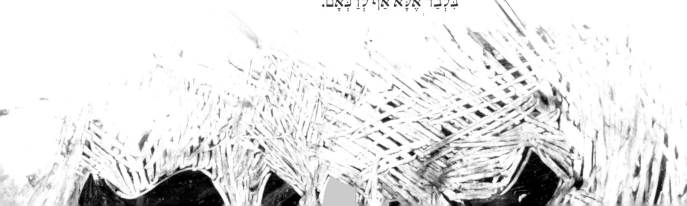

The "Sarajevo Haggadah," one of the world's finest examples of a Jewish illuminated manuscript, is created in Barcelona. It is taken out of Spain by Jewish refugees after the expulsion of 1492, resurfaces in Italy in the 16th century, and is sold to Sarajevo's National Museum in 1894. During World War II, the museum's director conceals the Haggadah from the Nazis by hiding it with a Muslim family. During the Bosnian civil war, in the midst of constant bombing from Serbian forces, the Haggadah is hidden by museum employees. Tonight it is in the Zemaljiski Museum in Sarajevo.

וַיָּרֵעוּ אֹתָנוּ הַמִּצְרִים. שֶׁעָשׂוּ אֹתָנוּ רָעִים, כְּמָה שֶׁנֶּאֱמַר: הָבָה נִתְחַכְּמָה לוֹ, פֶּן יִרְבֶּה, וְהָיָה כִּי תִקְרֶאנָה מִלְחָמָה וְנוֹסַף גַּם הוּא עַל שׂנְאֵינוּ, וְנִלְחַם בָּנוּ וְעָלָה מִן הָאָרֶץ.

דָּבָר אַחֵר: וַיָּרֵעוּ אֹתָנוּ הַמִּצְרִים. כְּפוּיֵי טוֹבָה הָיוּ, וְשִׁלְּמוּ רָעָה תַּחַת הַטּוֹבָה שֶׁעָשָׂה לָהֶם יוֹסֵף, כְּמָה שֶׁנֶּאֱמַר: וַיָּקָם מֶלֶךְ חָדָשׁ עַל מִצְרַיִם אֲשֶׁר לֹא יָדַע אֶת יוֹסֵף. עָשָׂה אֶת עַצְמוֹ כְּאִלּוּ לֹא יָדַע אֶת יוֹסֵף.

וַיְעַנּוּנוּ. כְּמָה שֶׁנֶּאֱמַר: וַיָּשִׂימוּ עָלָיו שָׂרֵי מִסִּים לְמַעַן עַנֹּתוֹ בְּסִבְלֹתָם, וַיִּבֶן עָרֵי מִסְכְּנוֹת לְפַרְעֹה, אֶת פִּתֹם וְאֶת רַעַמְסֵס.

וַיִּתְּנוּ עָלֵינוּ עֲבוֹדָה קָשָׁה. כְּמָה שֶׁנֶּאֱמַר: וַיַּעֲבִדוּ מִצְרַיִם אֶת בְּנֵי יִשְׂרָאֵל בְּפָרֶךְ.

דָּבָר אַחֵר: וַיִּתְּנוּ עָלֵינוּ עֲבֹדָה קָשָׁה. שֶׁהָיוּ מַחֲלִיפִין מְלֶאכֶת גָּדוֹל לְקָטָן וּמְלֶאכֶת קָטָן לְגָדוֹל, מְלֶאכֶת זָקֵן לְבָחוּר וּמְלֶאכֶת בָּחוּר לְזָקֵן. הֲרֵי זוֹ עֲבֹדָה שֶׁאֵין לָהּ קִצְבָה, שֶׁלֹּא רָצוּ לְשַׁעֲבֵד אֹתָם בִּלְבַד אֶלָּא אַף לְדַכְּאָם.

Circa 1380

In southern
Germany, a scribe
creates the oldest
surviving Ashkenazi
illuminated
Haggadah. In a twist
on the conventions
of illuminated
manuscripts, he
gives many of the
human figures
birds' heads.

*A*nd they did us evil, those Egyptians. They made us seem malevolent, as it is written: *Behold, the nation of the children of Israel has become too many and too massive for us. Let us find a solution for this before they further multiply. And if war is declared, they will align themselves with our enemies, and they will battle against us, and escape from the land.*

> An alternate reading: *And they did us evil, those Egyptians.* They were ungrateful. They paid back in wickedness the patronage Joseph gave them, as it is written: *And a new king, who did not know Joseph, was installed over Egypt.* Really, it was the same king acting *as if* he did not know Joseph.

And they tortured us. As it is written: *And they installed over the nation taskmasters for the express purpose of making them suffer with their burdens. The nation built treasure cities for Pharaoh, both Pitom and Ramesses.*

And they saddled us with punishing work. As it is written: *And the Egyptians worked the children of Israel with a vigor that wore at their bones.*

> An alternate reading: *And they saddled us with punishing work.* They were exchanging labors, foisting tasks for the big on the little, and tasks for the little on the big. Tasks fit for the old were put on the young, and the young boy's task was placed on the old man. It was a grinding work without end, born not only from wanting to enslave them, but in the hopes of grinding down their hearts.

וַנִּצְעַק אֶל יהוה

וַנִּצְעַק אֶל יהוה אֱלֹהֵי אֲבֹתֵינוּ, וַיִּשְׁמַע יהוה אֶת קֹלֵנוּ, וַיַּרְא אֶת עָנְיֵנוּ וְאֶת עֲמָלֵנוּ וְאֶת לַחֲצֵנוּ.

וַנִּצְעַק אֶל יהוה אֱלֹהֵי אֲבֹתֵינוּ. כְּמָה שֶׁנֶּאֱמַר: וַיְהִי בַיָּמִים הָרַבִּים הָהֵם וַיָּמָת מֶלֶךְ מִצְרַיִם וַיֵּאָנְחוּ בְנֵי יִשְׂרָאֵל מִן הָעֲבֹדָה וַיִּזְעָקוּ, וַתַּעַל שַׁוְעָתָם אֶל הָאֱלֹהִים מִן הָעֲבֹדָה.

דָּבָר אַחֵר: אֱלֹהֵי אֲבֹתֵינוּ. בִּזְכוּת אָבוֹת נִגְאֲלוּ מִמִּצְרָיִם.

1387

Geoffrey Chaucer begins his epic poem "The Canterbury Tales." Although Jews had been expelled from England a century earlier, Chaucer has his character of the prioress tell a tale of the murder of a Christian child by Jews, reminding her fellow pilgrims of the martyrdom of St. Hugh of Lincoln in 1255: "Yonge hugh of lyncoln, slayn also,/ With cursed jewes."

*A*nd *we cried out to the Lord, God of our fathers, and the Lord heard our voices, and He saw our torture and our toil and the great pressure upon us.*

And we cried out to the Lord, God of our fathers. As it is written: *And it came to pass during that interminable time that the ruler of Egypt died, and the children of Israel did groan from their toil—and they screamed out, and raised a cry to God from under the weight of their work.*

An alternate reading: *God of our fathers.* On the merit of our fathers we were liberated from Egypt.

The new technology
of the printing press
is used to create a
Haggadah for the
first time when
Solomon ben Moses
Alkabez publishes
a new edition in
Guadalajara, Spain.
In the following
century, there are 25
new editions of the
Haggadah; in the
17th century, 37; in
the 18th, 234; in the
19th, 1,269; and in
the 20th, over 1,000.

וַיִּשְׁמַע יהוה אֶת קֹלֵנוּ.
כְּמָה שֶׁנֶּאֱמַר: וַיִּשְׁמַע אֱלֹהִים אֶת
נַאֲקָתָם, וַיִּזְכֹּר אֱלֹהִים אֶת בְּרִיתוֹ, אֶת
אַבְרָהָם אֶת יִצְחָק וְאֶת יַעֲקֹב.

וַיַּרְא אֶת עָנְיֵנוּ. זוֹ פְּרִישׁוּת
דֶּרֶךְ אֶרֶץ, כְּמָה שֶׁנֶּאֱמַר: וַיַּרְא
אֱלֹהִים אֶת בְּנֵי יִשְׂרָאֵל,
וַיֵּדַע אֱלֹהִים.

דָּבָר אַחֵר: וַיִּשְׁמַע יהוה
אֶת קֹלֵנוּ. כְּמָה שֶׁנֶּאֱמַר:
רָאֹה רָאִיתִי אֶת עֳנִי עַמִּי
אֲשֶׁר בְּמִצְרָיִם וְאֶת צַעֲקָתָם
שָׁמַעְתִּי מִפְּנֵי נֹגְשָׂיו,
כִּי יָדַעְתִּי אֶת מַכְאֹבָיו.
וָאֵרֵד לְהַצִּילוֹ מִיַּד מִצְרַיִם
וּלְהַעֲלֹתוֹ מִן הָאָרֶץ הַהִיא.
וְנֶאֱמַר: עִמּוֹ אָנֹכִי בְצָרָה.
וְנֶאֱמַר בְּכָל צָרָתָם לוֹ צָר.

דָּבָר אַחֵר:
וַיַּרְא. מָה רָאָה? שֶׁהָיוּ בְּנֵי
יִשְׂרָאֵל מְרַחֲמִים זֶה עַל זֶה.
הָיָה אֶחָד מֵהֶם מַשְׁלִים אֶת
סְכוּם הַלְּבֵנִים שֶׁלּוֹ, וְהָיָה
מְסַיֵּעַ לַחֲבֵרוֹ.

אֶת עָנְיֵנוּ. גָּזְרוּ עֲלֵיהֶם
אֲנָשִׁים יָלִינוּ בַּשָּׂדֶה
וְהַנָּשִׁים בָּעִיר, כְּדֵי לְמַעֲטָן
בִּפְרִיָּה וְרִבְיָה. וְנָשֶׁיהֶם
מְחַמְּמוֹת לָהֶם חַמִּין
וּמְבִיאוֹת לְבַעֲלֵיהֶן כָּל
מַאֲכָל וּמִשְׁתֶּה, וּמְנַחֲמוֹת
אֹתָם וְאוֹמְרוֹת: לְעוֹלָם לֹא
מִשְׁתַּעְבְּדִין בָּנוּ,
סוֹף הַקָּדוֹשׁ בָּרוּךְ הוּא
גּוֹאֵל אֹתָנוּ.
מִתּוֹךְ כָּךְ בָּאִים עֲלֵיהֶן
וּפָרִים וְרָבִים. מִכָּאן,
שֶׁבִּזְכוּת נָשִׁים צִדְקָנִיּוֹת
שֶׁהָיוּ בְּאוֹתוֹ הַדּוֹר נִגְאֲלוּ
יִשְׂרָאֵל מִמִּצְרָיִם.

1492

Jews are forced out of Spain by Ferdinand and Isabella's decree of March 30, giving them four months to convert or leave the country. The Andalusian port of Cádiz, crowded with throngs of boats carrying Jewish refugees, leaves no room for Christopher Columbus to begin his journey to the Indies, and he resorts to departing from Palos de la Frontera instead.

And the Lord heard our voices. As it is written: *And God heard their wailing, and God remembered His covenant, His Abraham, His Isaac, His Jacob.*

An alternate reading: *And the Lord heard our voices.* As it is said: "*I saw and have seen the impoverishment of my nation in Egypt, and I heard their scream in the face of their oppressors—because of this I knew their pain. And I went down to wrest them from Egypt's grasp, and to lift them out from that land.*" And it is written: "*With them I am one in misery.*" And it is written: "*The entirety of their misery, was for Him misery.*"

And He saw our torture. This was a break with the natural order, as it is written: *And God saw the children of Israel, and God knew.*

An alternate reading: *And He saw.* What did He see? That the children of Israel had compassion, one for the other. When one of them would fulfill his quota of brickmaking, he would then help finish that of his friend.

Our torture. They decreed that the men must lodge in the fields, and the women in the city, in order to contain their fruitfulness and abundance. And their wives warmed hearty dishes and brought them to their husbands—copious food and drink. And they would console them, saying: "Never will they manage to make the slavery part of us, for in the end the Holy One, Blessed is He, will redeem us." This spurred them to their men, and they were fruitful and abundant. From this we learn, it was on the merits of the righteous women of that generation that Israel was liberated from Egypt.

וְאֶת עֲמָלֵנוּ. אֵלּוּ הַבָּנִים.
כְּמָה שֶׁנֶּאֱמַר: כָּל הַבֵּן הַיִּלּוֹד
הַיְאֹרָה תַּשְׁלִיכֻהוּ, וְכָל
הַבַּת תְּחַיּוּן. הָיוּ יִשְׂרָאֵל מָלִים
אֶת בְּנֵיהֶם בְּמִצְרַיִם. אָמְרוּ לָהֶם
מִצְרִיִּים: לָמָה אַתֶּם מָלִים אוֹתָם,
שֶׁלְּאַחַר שָׁעָה אָנוּ מַשְׁלִיכִים אֹתָם
בַּנָּהָר? אָמְרוּ לָהֶם: אַף עַל פִּי כֵן
נָמוֹל אוֹתָם.

וְאֶת לַחֲצֵנוּ – זוֹ הַדְּחַק,
כְּמָה שֶׁנֶּאֱמַר, וְגַם רָאִיתִי אֶת הַלַּחַץ
אֲשֶׁר מִצְרַיִם לֹחֲצִים אֹתָם.

דָּבָר אַחֵר: וְאֶת לַחֲצֵנוּ.
זֶה הַתֶּבֶן. שֶׁפַּרְעֹה גָזַר:
לֹא תֹאסִפוּן לָתֵת תֶּבֶן
לָעָם לִלְבֹּן הַלְּבֵנִים כִּתְמוֹל
שִׁלְשֹׁם. הֵם יֵלְכוּ וְקֹשְׁשׁוּ
לָהֶם תֶּבֶן. הָיוּ בָּאִים הַמִּצְרִים
וּמוֹנִים אֶת הַלְּבֵנִים וְנִמְצְאוּ
חֲסֵרוֹת. וְשׁוֹטְרֵי יִשְׂרָאֵל לֹא
הָיוּ מוֹסְרִים אֶת בְּנֵי יִשְׂרָאֵל
בְּיַד הַמִּצְרִים. מָסְרוּ עַצְמָם
עַל בְּנֵי יִשְׂרָאֵל וְסָבְלוּ מַכּוֹת
כְּדֵי לְהָקֵל מֵעֲלֵיהֶם.

1505

Writing from Venice, the Spanish refugee Isaac Abravanel asks, "What benefit have we derived from the exodus from Egypt, in view of the fact that we are once again in exile?"

1500

The world's Jewish population is approximately 900,000, or about 0.2% of the total global population.

A nd our toil. Our sons. As it is written: *Every son that is born, toss to the river, and every daughter, let live.* Israel was circumcising its sons in Egypt. The Egyptians asked: "Why are you circumcising them, when an hour later we will be throwing them into the river?" They replied: "Nevertheless, we will circumcise them."

And the great pressure upon us. Our stress. As it is said: *And I, too, see the pressure Egypt exerts upon them.*

An alternate reading: *And the great pressure upon us.* This alludes to the straw. As Pharaoh decreed: *Gather no more straw for that nation for the bricking of bricks, as you had before. Let them go out and reap straw for themselves.* The Egyptians would come and tally the bricks and find shortfalls. Yet the enforcers of Israel would not relinquish the children of Israel into the hands of the Egyptians. Instead, they sacrificed themselves for the children of Israel, suffering blows so as to ease for the others what was upon them.

God forgets. A shocking idea: God chose us, and then forgot us. Only by wailing did we remind him of our existence. But God's problem is our problem as well. We're masters of forgetting: about prejudice and unfairness, wars and genocides, hunger and misery. We're busy; we're overwhelmed; we're callous. So what reminds us of injustice in the world? Wailing. Protest. Complaining. Suffering in silence is not a Jewish virtue. Complaining is a Jewish virtue, because dissatisfaction is a particularly Jewish characteristic. Sometimes we are dissatisfied by trivial matters, by issues of money and status and luxury. But one of the joys of being Jewish is membership in a group that is eternally dissatisfied with the way things are. We are, at our core, a messianic people. We dream of a better time, when the entire world will make the journey from slavery to freedom. And how will that journey begin? By opening our mouths. Wherever people gather to express dissatisfaction with the way things are—on the environment, on taxes, on immigration, on civil rights and social policy and foreign policy—you will find Jews leading the fight. Often, you will find Jews leading both sides of the same dispute. It was remarkable to watch the struggle over the Bush administration's decision to go to war in Iraq: Jewish advisers to Bush were key in making the case, while Jews in Congress and in the media led the charge against intervention. At times, the argument took on the appearance of an intramural dispute. Throughout history, Jews have been agitators for change. Jews are disproportionately active in the politics of dozens of countries; in America, more than 10 percent of the U.S. Senate is Jewish (Jews make up 2 percent of the population), and Jews register to vote, and turn out to vote, in much higher percentages than any other group.

The question arises, Do Jews who agitate so ardently for change do so as Jews, or *because* they are Jews? Is there something embedded in the Jewish cultural DNA—the memory of Moses' calling, perhaps—that sparks a desire to change the world? Or is it just coincidence?

The most theologically shocking moment in Exodus is not when God appears in the burning bush, or splits the Sea of Reeds, or even when he gives the Ten

Commandments at Sinai. It is when God remembers his covenant with Israel.

How can a God who was so close at hand in Genesis that he spoke directly to Abraham, overheard Sarah laughing, and wrestled with Jacob "face to face," be so far away when their descendants are enslaved in Egypt? The "peshat," or plain sense, of Exodus suggests an answer that is both simple and horrifying: God, who spent the better part of Genesis cultivating the people of Israel, has, by only the second chapter of Exodus, forgotten that they are his nation and, therefore, his responsibility. Here, stripped bare, lies the theological root of one of the deepest fears in the collective Jewish psyche, the fear of forgetting and being forgotten.

And yet, according to the Haggadah, there is a remedy for God's amnesia: Israel's voice, our voice. Just as, later in Exodus, Moses commands Israel to "remember this day on which you departed from Egypt, from the house of bondage, for with a strong hand God removed you from here," so, too, if we want a relationship with God, we must remind him, with wails if necessary, to remember his covenant with us. But what would those wails look like today? And how would we know if God heard them?

"And the Lord heard our voices."

As it is written: *"And God heard their wailing, and God remembered His covenant, His Abraham, His Isaac, His Jacob."*

God, who supposedly knows everything, needs to be reminded of a promise He made with our ancestors. This is disconcerting—a word which here means "cause for much argument among rabbis and peasants alike"—but not surprising. All of us have forgotten about promises we have made, even promises that are very important to us, and that are still very important to the people to whom we've promised them. These people may be wailing right this very minute, hoping that we remember whatever it is that we promised. Perhaps we promised to help them with something, but then the task was so dull that we put it aside. Perhaps we promised to be kind to them, but then we became interested in other people instead. Or perhaps we simply promised to keep thinking about them, but we have forgotten about these people until this very moment, because it is so much more interesting to think about ourselves and our own problems.

It is entirely possible that God, too, would rather think of Himself, and His own problems. When we suspect this to be the case, Jewish tradition encourages us to wail, often in Hebrew. But we might also stop wailing for a moment and listen instead. We might think of promises we have made and have not kept, or promises we ought to have made but didn't, and while we're thinking of this, we might hear the wailing of others, some of whom may be trapped beneath the floors of this very room.

Playground

Kafka once wrote in his journal: "You can hold yourself back from the sufferings of the world. That is something you are free to do and it accords with your nature. But perhaps this very holding back is the one suffering you could avoid."

The "you" that Kafka is addressing might be himself, or it might be each of us. But it also could be—and here's the stunner—the God of Exodus Himself. It accords with His nature, too, to hold Himself back from the sufferings of the world, something He is quite free to do, and apparently does rather well, withdrawing into the godlike completeness of His remove until He is wrenched out of it by receiving suffering humanity's revelation, which comes in the form of wails.

Library

Wails come straight from a soul stripped down to the bone, and they are always a revelation. To hear someone's wails is to see a self revealed in ways usually kept hidden, driven by extremes to dropping poses and speech. Wailing draws the hearer into an intimate space, whether the hearer wants to be there or not—and the God of this passage would appear not to have wanted to be there, and we can all sympathize with His desire to be anywhere else. But then He is there, summoned out of His remoteness by revelation. Revelation is generally presented as proceeding from God to man. Here the revelation travels in the opposite direction. The God of Exodus is not so unlimitedly free after all. He is bound by moral obligations, even if it takes an unwelcome revelation to remind Him.

Tonight we dream of freedom. But should we dream of some godlike freedom that draws us ever more distantly away from one another, self-contained in our preoccupations with self-image and the ways and means for self-projection and self-protection, then this passage reminds us of what we chance to lose. It is in the intimate spaces that the unwelcome and necessary revelations come, and we withdraw from those intimate spaces at our peril.

A nd the Lord lifted us out of Egypt in the mighty hand of an outstretched arm, with an awesome spectacle, with signs and undeniable wonders.

Michelangelo
completes his
sculpture of Moses,
which is installed in
Rome's San Pietro
in Vincoli church.
In keeping with a
misinterpretation
of Exodus 34:29-30
by Latin translators
of the Bible, who
rendered the Hebrew
word for "rays" of
light as "horns,"
Michelangelo gives
his Moses a pair on
the top of his head.

In Frankfurt am
Main, the German
friar Thomas Murner
publishes a Latin
Haggadah—the first
full translation of
the Haggadah in any
language—in part
to counter Christian
attacks on Passover.

וַיּוֹצִאֵנוּ יהוה מִמִּצְרַיִם, בְּיָד חֲזָקָה וּבִזְרֹעַ
נְטוּיָה וּבְמֹרָא גָּדֹל, וּבְאֹתוֹת וּבְמֹפְתִים.

וַיּוֹצִאֵנוּ יהוה מִמִּצְרָיִם. לֹא עַל יְדֵי מַלְאָךְ וְלֹא עַל יְדֵי שָׂרָף וְלֹא עַל יְדֵי שָׁלִיחַ, אֶלָּא הַקָּדוֹשׁ בָּרוּךְ הוּא בִּכְבוֹדוֹ וּבְעַצְמוֹ, שֶׁנֶּאֱמַר: וְעָבַרְתִּי בְאֶרֶץ מִצְרַיִם בַּלַּיְלָה הַזֶּה, וְהִכֵּיתִי כָל בְּכוֹר בְּאֶרֶץ מִצְרַיִם מֵאָדָם וְעַד בְּהֵמָה, וּבְכָל אֱלֹהֵי מִצְרַיִם אֶעֱשֶׂה שְׁפָטִים, אֲנִי יהוה.

וְעָבַרְתִּי בְאֶרֶץ מִצְרַיִם בַּלַּיְלָה הַזֶּה. אֲנִי וְלֹא מַלְאָךְ. וְהִכֵּיתִי כָל בְּכוֹר בְּאֶרֶץ מִצְרַיִם. אֲנִי וְלֹא שָׂרָף. וּבְכָל אֱלֹהֵי מִצְרַיִם אֶעֱשֶׂה שְׁפָטִים. אֲנִי וְלֹא הַשָּׁלִיחַ. אֲנִי יהוה. אֲנִי הוּא וְלֹא אַחֵר.

And the Lord lifted us out of Egypt. Not by the hands of an Angel of Man, and not by the hands of an Angel Alight, and not by the hands of a Messenger Angel, but rather it was done by the Holy One, Blessed is He; done by His Glorious Self—and by Himself, as it is said: *And I will cross through the land of Egypt on this night, and I will strike every firstborn in the land of Egypt, from man to beast, and I—on all the gods of Egypt—will deliver judgment. I am the Lord!*

And I will cross through the land of Egypt on this night.
I and not an Angel of Man.
And I will strike every firstborn in the land of Egypt.
I and not an Angel Alight.
And I—on all the gods of Egypt—will deliver judgment.
I and not a Messenger Angel.
I am the Lord! I am Him and no other.

In his family's
majolica workshop
in Ferrara, Italy,
Isaac Azulai puts
the final touches
on a seder plate by
painting the Hebrew
phrase "A woman
of valor is a friend
to her husband" in
the center. Tonight
the plate is in the
Israel Museum in
Jerusalem.

בְּיָד חֲזָקָה - זוֹ הַדֶּבֶר כְּמָה שֶׁנֶּאֱמַר: הִנֵּה יַד יהוה הוֹיָה בְּמִקְנְךָ אֲשֶׁר בַּשָּׂדֶה, בַּסּוּסִים בַּחֲמֹרִים בַּגְּמַלִּים בַּבָּקָר וּבַצֹּאן, דֶּבֶר כָּבֵד מְאֹד.

וּבִזְרֹעַ נְטוּיָה - זוֹ הַחֶרֶב, כְּמָה שֶׁנֶּאֱמַר: וְחַרְבּוֹ שְׁלוּפָה בְּיָדוֹ, נְטוּיָה עַל יְרוּשָׁלָיִם.

דָּבָר אַחֵר: בְּיָד חֲזָקָה וּבִזְרֹעַ נְטוּיָה. כְּשֶׁמָּרְרוּ הַמִּצְרִים אֶת חַיֵּי אֲבֹתֵינוּ, אָמַר הַקָּדוֹשׁ בָּרוּךְ הוּא: וְגָאַלְתִּי אֶתְכֶם, שֶׁנֶּאֱמַר: וְהוֹצֵאתִי אֶתְכֶם מִתַּחַת סִבְלֹת מִצְרַיִם, וְהִצַּלְתִּי אֶתְכֶם מֵעֲבֹדָתָם, וְגָאַלְתִּי אֶתְכֶם בִּזְרֹעַ נְטוּיָה וּבִשְׁפָטִים גְּדֹלִים. וְלָקַחְתִּי אֶתְכֶם לִי לְעָם וְהָיִיתִי לָכֶם לֵאלֹהִים, וִידַעְתֶּם כִּי אֲנִי יהוה אֱלֹהֵיכֶם.

וּבְמֹרָא גָדֹל. זֶה גִּלּוּי שְׁכִינָה, כְּמָה שֶׁנֶּאֱמַר: אוֹ הֲנִסָּה אֱלֹהִים לָבוֹא לָקַחַת לוֹ גוֹי מִקֶּרֶב גּוֹי, בְּמַסֹּת בְּאֹתֹת וּבְמוֹפְתִים וּבְמִלְחָמָה, וּבְיָד חֲזָקָה וּבִזְרוֹעַ נְטוּיָה וּבְמוֹרָאִים גְּדֹלִים, כְּכֹל אֲשֶׁר עָשָׂה לָכֶם יהוה אֱלֹהֵיכֶם בְּמִצְרַיִם לְעֵינֶיךָ.

After an outbreak of the plague in Lublin, Poland, the printer Kalonymus ben Mordecai Yafe flees to the town of Bistrowitz and publishes a Haggadah. In the book's preface, he uses Numbers 17:13 to explain its origins: "And he stood between the dead and the living; and the plague was stayed."

"Chad Gadya," a traditional children's song, becomes a standard element of the Passover seder when it is distributed in printed form in a Haggadah published in Prague.

*I*n the mighty hand. This alludes to the pestilence, as it is written: *Behold, the hand of the Lord is on your livestock in the field, on the horses, on the donkeys, on your camels, on your cattle and on your sheep—a brutal pestilence.*

Of an outstretched arm. This alludes to the sword, as it is written: *And his sword is unsheathed in his hand, outstretched in judgment over Jerusalem.*

An alternate reading: *In the mighty hand of an outstretched arm.* When the Egyptians embittered the lives of our fathers, the Holy One, Blessed is He, said: *And I will redeem you.* As it is said: *And I will lift you out from under the millstone that is Egypt and I will rescue you from their tyranny, and I will redeem you with an outstretched arm and formidable judgments. And I will take you for myself as a nation, and I will be for you as a God, and you will know that I am the Lord God-of-You.*

And with an awesome spectacle. This is the Divine Presence in revealed form, as it is said: *Has God ever attempted to come take for Himself nation from the belly of nation, with phenomenal trials, with signs and undeniable wonders, with war and with the mighty hand of an outstretched arm, with awesome spectacles and—like everything else done for you in Egypt by the Lord God-of-You—all this before your very eyes?*

וּבְאֹתוֹת. זֶה הַמַּטֶּה, כְּמָה שֶׁנֶּאֱמַר: וְאֶת הַמַּטֶּה הַזֶּה תִּקַּח בְּיָדֶךָ אֲשֶׁר תַּעֲשֶׂה בּוֹ אֶת הָאֹתֹת.

דָּבָר אַחֵר: וּבְאֹתוֹת. אֵלּוּ מִצְוֹת יהוה, שֶׁהֵם אוֹת לְעוֹלָם שֶׁהוּא אֵל מַצִּיל וּמוֹשִׁיעַ, וְזִכָּרוֹן בְּכָל דּוֹר וָדוֹר לַבְּרִית שֶׁבֵּין הַקָּדוֹשׁ בָּרוּךְ הוּא לְבֵין עַמּוֹ, כְּמָה שֶׁנֶּאֱמַר: וְהָיָה לְךָ לְאוֹת עַל יָדְךָ וּלְזִכָּרוֹן בֵּין עֵינֶיךָ, לְמַעַן תִּהְיֶה תּוֹרַת יהוה בְּפִיךָ, כִּי בְּיָד חֲזָקָה הוֹצִאֲךָ יהוה מִמִּצְרָיִם.

וּבְמֹפְתִים - זֶה הַדָּם, כְּמָה שֶׁנֶּאֱמַר: נָתַתִּי מוֹפְתִים בַּשָּׁמַיִם וּבָאָרֶץ: דָּם וָאֵשׁ וְתִימְרוֹת עָשָׁן.

דָּבָר אַחֵר: בְּיָד חֲזָקָה, שְׁתַּיִם. וּבִזְרֹעַ נְטוּיָה, שְׁתַּיִם. וּבְמֹרָא גָדֹל, שְׁתַּיִם. וּבְאֹתוֹת שְׁתַּיִם. וּבְמֹפְתִים שְׁתַּיִם.

1599

To cater to the
multilingual
population of
Venice's Jewish
ghetto, a new
Haggadah features
three columns of
translation: one in
Yiddish for Central
European Jews, one
in Judeo-Italian for
locals, and one in
Ladino for the city's
growing community
of Spanish exiles and
their descendants.

And with signs. This alludes to the staff, as it is said: *Take this staff in your hand, and use it to perform the signs.*

An alternate reading: *With signs.* These are the mitzvot of the Lord, which serve as an eternal sign of a God rescuing and redeeming, and as a memory to ferry throughout the generations, a covenant between the Holy One, Blessed is He, and His nation, as it is said: *And it shall be for you a sign on your hand and a remembrance between your eyes, so that the Lord's teaching will fill your mouth, for it was with a mighty hand that the Lord lifted you out of Egypt.*

While saying "blood," "fire," and "pillars of smoke," use a finger to transfer a drop of wine from the cup to the dinner plate —one drop for each phrase.

And with undeniable wonders. This is the blood, as it is said: *And I will place undeniable wonders in the heavens and on the earth,* **blood** *and* **fire** *and* **pillars of smoke.**

An alternate reading: *In the mighty hand,* two plagues. *Of an outstretched arm,* two plagues. *With an awesome spectacle,* two plagues. *With signs,* two plagues. *And undeniable wonders,* two plagues.

אֵלּוּ עֶשֶׂר מַכּוֹת
שֶׁהֵבִיא הַקָּדוֹשׁ בָּרוּךְ הוּא עַל הַמִּצְרִים
בְּמִצְרַיִם וְאֵלּוּ הֵן:

1623

In Flanders, a deserter from the Spanish army is arrested for claiming to be the Wandering Jew.

These are the ten plagues that the Holy One, Blessed is He, brought upon the Egyptians in Egypt:

While saying the name of each of the plagues, use a finger to transfer a drop of wine from the cup to the dinner plate.

Blood, frogs, lice, a maelstrom of beasts, pestilence, boils, and hail-full-of-fire, locusts, a clotted darkness—too thick to pass. The killing of the firstborn.

דָּם, צְפַרְדֵּעַ, כִּנִּים, עָרוֹב, דֶּבֶר, שְׁחִין, בָּרָד, אַרְבֶּה, חֹשֶׁךְ, מַכַּת בְּכוֹרוֹת.

While saying, "Dtzah," "Adash," and "B'achab," use a finger to transfer a drop of wine from the cup to the dinner plate—one drop for each word.

Rabbi Yehuda formed them into a mnemonic: **Dtzah, Adash, B'achab.**

רַבִּי יְהוּדָה הָיָה נוֹתֵן בָּהֶם סִמָּנִים: דְּצַ"ךְ עַדַ"שׁ בְּאַחַ"ב.

The diarist Glueckel
bas Judah is born
in the port of
Hamburg in northern
Germany. When she
is two, Hamburg's
Jewish community
is expelled from
the city, and her
family takes refuge
in nearby Altona
before returning to
Hamburg nine years
later. At twelve, she
is betrothed and
moves to Hameln to
join her husband's
family, raises
twelve children,
and assists her
husband in running
his trading firm. She
begins writing her
autobiography after
his death in 1689.
In 1699, she marries
Cerf Levy and moves
with him to Metz,
France, where she
lives until her death
in 1724.

רַבִּי יוֹסֵי הַגְּלִילִי אוֹמֵר: מִנַּיִן אַתָּה אוֹמֵר שֶׁלָּקוּ
הַמִּצְרִים בְּמִצְרַיִם עֶשֶׂר מַכּוֹת וְעַל הַיָּם לָקוּ חֲמִשִּׁים
מַכּוֹת? בְּמִצְרַיִם מָה הוּא אוֹמֵר, וַיֹּאמְרוּ הַחַרְטֻמִּים אֶל פַּרְעֹה,
אֶצְבַּע אֱלֹהִים הוּא, וְעַל הַיָּם מָה הוּא אוֹמֵר, וַיַּרְא יִשְׂרָאֵל אֶת הַיָּד הַגְּדֹלָה
אֲשֶׁר עָשָׂה יהוה בְּמִצְרַיִם, וַיִּירְאוּ הָעָם אֶת יהוה, וַיַּאֲמִינוּ בַּיהוה
וּבְמֹשֶׁה עַבְדּוֹ. כַּמָּה לָקוּ בְאֶצְבַּע? עֶשֶׂר מַכּוֹת. אֱמוֹר מֵעַתָּה: בְּמִצְרַיִם
לָקוּ עֶשֶׂר מַכּוֹת וְעַל הַיָּם לָקוּ חֲמִשִּׁים מַכּוֹת.

רַבִּי אֱלִיעֶזֶר אוֹמֵר: מִנַּיִן שֶׁכָּל מַכָּה וּמַכָּה שֶׁהֵבִיא
הַקָּדוֹשׁ בָּרוּךְ הוּא עַל הַמִּצְרִים בְּמִצְרַיִם הָיְתָה שֶׁל אַרְבַּע
מַכּוֹת? שֶׁנֶּאֱמַר, יְשַׁלַּח בָּם חֲרוֹן אַפּוֹ, עֶבְרָה, וָזַעַם, וְצָרָה - מִשְׁלַחַת
מַלְאֲכֵי רָעִים. עֶבְרָה, אַחַת. וָזַעַם, שְׁתַּיִם. וְצָרָה, שָׁלֹשׁ. מִשְׁלַחַת
מַלְאֲכֵי רָעִים, אַרְבַּע. אֱמוֹר מֵעַתָּה, בְּמִצְרַיִם לָקוּ אַרְבָּעִים מַכּוֹת,
וְעַל הַיָּם לָקוּ מָאתַיִם מַכּוֹת.

רַבִּי עֲקִיבָא אוֹמֵר. מִנַּיִן שֶׁכָּל מַכָּה וּמַכָּה שֶׁהֵבִיא
הַקָּדוֹשׁ בָּרוּךְ הוּא עַל הַמִּצְרִים בְּמִצְרַיִם הָיְתָה שֶׁל חָמֵשׁ
מַכּוֹת? שֶׁנֶּאֱמַר, יְשַׁלַּח בָּם חֲרוֹן אַפּוֹ, עֶבְרָה, וָזַעַם, וְצָרָה - מִשְׁלַחַת
מַלְאֲכֵי רָעִים. חֲרוֹן אַפּוֹ, אַחַת. עֶבְרָה, שְׁתַּיִם. וָזַעַם, שָׁלֹשׁ.
וְצָרָה, אַרְבַּע. מִשְׁלַחַת מַלְאֲכֵי רָעִים, חָמֵשׁ.
אֱמוֹר מֵעַתָּה, בְּמִצְרַיִם לָקוּ חֲמִשִּׁים מַכּוֹת וְעַל הַיָּם לָקוּ חֲמִשִּׁים
וּמָאתַיִם מַכּוֹת.

A Livorno Haggadah is printed in Spanish for former Conversos—Jews who converted to Christianity during the Inquisition but continued to practice elements of Judaism in secret. Since the new Jews know only fragments of Jewish rituals, the Haggadah includes instructions for how to make charoset: "Take apples or pears, cooked in water; hazelnuts or almonds; shelled chestnuts or walnuts; figs or raisins; and after cooking, grind them thoroughly and dissolve them in the strongest wine vinegar that can be found. Then mix in a bit of brick dust, in memory of the bricks which our fathers made in Egypt."

Rabbi Yossi ha-Galili said: How do we come to say that the Egyptians were struck with ten plagues in Egypt, and struck with fifty plagues by the sea? In reference to Egypt, what does it say? *And the magicians said to Pharaoh, "It is the finger of God!"* In reference to the sea, what does it say? *And Israel saw the massive hand that the Lord used against Egypt, and the nation revered the Lord, and had faith in the Lord, and in Moses His servant.* So how many were they struck with when God was using only one finger? Ten plagues. Let it be said from now on: In Egypt they were stricken with ten plagues, and by the sea stricken with fifty plagues.

Rabbi Eliezer said: How do we come to say that each and every plague that the Holy One, Blessed is He, visited on the Egyptians in Egypt was composed of four plagues? As it is written: *And He delivered upon them His wrath, furious, rageful and misery-making—a covey of evil angels. Fury,* one. *And rage,* two. *And misery,* three. *A covey of evil angels,* four. Let it be said from now on: In Egypt they were stricken with forty plagues, and by the sea stricken with two hundred plagues.

Rabbi Akiva said: How do you come to say that each and every plague that the Holy One, Blessed is He, visited on the Egyptians in Egypt was composed of five plagues? As it is written: *And He delivered upon them His wrath, furious, rageful and misery-making—a covey of evil angels. His wrath,* one. *Fury,* two. *Rage,* three. *And misery,* four. *A covey of evil angels,* five. Let it be said from now on: In Egypt they were stricken with fifty plagues, and by the sea stricken with fifty and two hundred plagues.

The Holy One, blessed be He, does not rejoice in the downfall of the wicked…Rabbi Johanan taught, "The ministering angels wanted to sing hymns [when God closed the Sea of Reeds on the Egyptians, causing them to drown], but the Holy One, blessed be He, said, 'My creatures are being drowned in the sea, and you want to sing hymns?'" Babylonian Talmud Megillah 10b

Is it possible to have too much justice? Can the pursuit of justice lead us, and even God, astray?

House of Study

Before he sends the ten plagues to strike Egypt, God describes them to Moses as "judgments," or shefatim, a word that shares the same Hebrew root as mishpat, or "justice." The plagues, then, do not merely demonstrate God's awesome power but also his desire for justice, for a reckoning that will restore the balance that the Egyptians have violently undone through their persecution of the Israelites.

Of all the plagues, the final one is by far the most disturbing. It is also the one that most directly embodies a kind of unadulterated justice. At the beginning of Exodus, Pharaoh "commanded all of his people, saying 'Every boy that is born you shall throw into the Nile, but let every girl live.'" Now God tells Moses, "I will go through the land of Egypt and strike down every firstborn in the land of Egypt, both man and beast." It is as close to an eye for an eye that the ten plagues come. And in this narrow sense, it is just. But it is not right.

The rabbis teach us that along with justice there is another principle that guides God's actions. And that principle is mercy. Justice is achieved by finding a punishment that fits the crime. Like karma, it seeks to restore a kind of balance. But the relationship between justice and mercy is ideally one of imbalance. Mercy, according to the rabbis, should outweigh justice. The kabbalists go one step further. For them, justice that has been severed from mercy is the root of evil. And that is what the tenth and final plague looks like. Justice severed from mercy. The rabbis also teach us that the Jewish people have the power to ensure that God's mercy tempers the potential excesses of his justice. After being enslaved and nearly extinguished by the Egyptians, we can understand why our ancestors did not press God to show their oppressors mercy during the ten plagues. But we, their free descendants, must not rejoice over the punishment of the Egyptians. It is not a moment for singing.

It is one of the peculiarities of the Passover story that God sends ten plagues down on all of the Egyptians, not just the ones who were in favor of slavery.

It is likely that there were a fair number of Egyptians who said, "I see no reason to detain these Hebrew slaves any longer than we already have," and who nevertheless found themselves drinking blood instead of water. By the time frogs had hopped through the land, and gnats and flies had stung everything in sight, there were doubtless more Egyptians who said, "You know, I would rather do without slaves than have all of these terrible pests around," and who still suffered from pestilence and boils. By the time the threats came from the sky—hail, locusts, and darkness—there couldn't have been too many Egyptians who were in favor of keeping the Jews in bondage, except the stubborn Pharaoh, who only changed his mind when his own son, who by this point was probably an abolitionist—a word which here means "in favor of ending slavery if only because he was sick of plagues"—was slaughtered as part of the tenth and final plague. It is likely that the entire Egyptian nation disagreed with the Pharaoh by that time, and yet it was the entire nation that was punished.

This is not fair, and Jewish tradition has us spill ten drops from the beverage of our choice when naming the plagues, in order to remember the suffering of the Egyptians. Of course, the pain and terror of ten plagues cannot compare with a glass that is slightly less full than it was originally, but tradition dictates that these ten drops are symbolic, a word which here means "a way of expressing how sorry we are about something that happened a long time ago and was not directly our fault." This symbolism may come in handy, so that some night at dinner you can say, "When I spilled grape juice all over your beautiful white tablecloth, it was not an accident, but my way of apologizing for various terrible things that have happened to innocent people."

Playground

Ten Plagues

The plagues that preceded the final calamity were terrible, but so, too, were the plagues that followed the departure of the Israelites from the land of Egypt.

Library

Those Egyptians who had survived the scourges could not escape the plague of their memories. Their nostrils sniffed the air as if fiery hailstones still burned the earth, and they moved slowly, their bodies recalling the immobility that had come when the darkness had covered them so thickly that they could not find their limbs. And while the plague of memory still raged, there came the plague of grieving, in every household a wail went up, each mother for her firstborn, and all the other mourners for their dead. And then the plague of doubt fell on them, when they considered that their gods had not been able to save them, and the high priests and magicians could not deliver them from their uncertainty. And then came the plague of helplessness, as the Egyptians wandered dazed through their unslaved homes and unslaved cities, and the plague of their shame, when they considered how it was that they had been brought so low and by whom, and the plague of blame for their Pharaoh, who had delivered them into their defeat, and the plague of hatred for the Israelites, wily and unworthy, whom they would never forgive, they swore it, pledged themselves to forever feed off the dream of vengeance, which was the plague that preceded the ninth, which was that of pure madness. But the bitterest of all was the tenth and final plague. It was only when the plague of remorse fell on the crushed Egyptians that they cried out for mercy, and that was the moment that the sweetness of mercy came to them at last.

It is one kind of moral victory to be rescued from wrongs that are done to us. It is another kind of moral victory to rescue ourselves by facing the wrongs that we do. Let some of the drops that we spill be for our own wrongdoing selves, grieving our hurtful mistakes, forgiving ourselves for our lack of moral perfection, remorseful but hopeful that we can learn and go on.

Our impulse is to run from this moment, to pretend that our merciful God has not transformed Himself into a God who snuffs out the lives of children. But this story exists for a

Nation

reason, and perhaps not the one often assumed. The plagues suffered by the Egyptians are meant not merely to serve as expedient metaphors. This is a political story, yes, but one with a harsh and morally problematical lesson about the price of freedom.

There is no such thing as an immaculate liberation. From time to time—in the Velvet Revolution of the former Czechoslovakia, for example—liberation has been achieved without the shedding of blood. But it is naïve to think that the defeat of evil comes without cost. Today, we retreat in disgust at the thought of collective punishment: Justice punishes the guilty and spares the innocent. And yet how else could we describe the plagues?

And don't we sometimes behave today as the God of Exodus behaved? Don't we impose sanctions on dictatorships and by so doing cause hardship for the guiltless? Haven't we made heroes of men who have deliberately taken the lives of thousands of innocents? Three of the most revered presidents in American history—Abraham Lincoln, Franklin Delano Roosevelt, and Harry Truman—inflicted merciless punishment on civilians. The causes they stood for were just, but did the innocent sufferers deserve their fate? Why did God harden Pharaoh's heart against the Jews, even after it seemed Pharaoh was ready to let them go? Did God want to make a point—"Don't even think of challenging me"? Why did America shower death on Nagasaki, when it seemed that the Japanese were readying themselves to surrender? Was the firebombing of German cities so necessary as to neutralize all moral qualms? The Exodus story ends in freedom for Jews; the Civil War ended with freedom for African-Americans; World War II ended with fascism utterly vanquished, and the death camps liberated. Can we say that the ends didn't justify the means?

1654

A boatload of Dutch Jews sails into the harbor of New York, then called New Amsterdam. They are refugees from the Dutch colony of Recife in Brazil, which had just been taken over by the Portuguese. Fearing the instatement of the Catholic Inquisition by the colony's new rulers, they fled north. Despite the objections of Peter Stuyvesant, the Dutch East India Company permits them to settle in New Amsterdam.

1657

Manasseh ben Israel, born Manoel Dias Soeiro in Portugal and leader of Amsterdam's Converso community, dies. The stamp he uses to mark his books is the image of a wanderer, bearing his possessions on his back, with a view of a distant city.

כַּמָּה מַעֲלוֹת טוֹבוֹת לַמָּקוֹם עָלֵינוּ.

With how many layers of goodness has God blessed us?

Uri Phoebus ben
Aaron Halevi
publishes a guide to
Passover in Yiddish
for Jews who don't
know Hebrew.

אִלּוּ הוֹצִיאָנוּ מִמִּצְרַיִם וְלֹא עָשָׂה בָהֶם שְׁפָטִים, דַּיֵּנוּ.

אִלּוּ עָשָׂה בָהֶם שְׁפָטִים וְלֹא עָשָׂה בֵאלֹהֵיהֶם, דַּיֵּנוּ.

אִלּוּ עָשָׂה בֵאלֹהֵיהֶם וְלֹא הָרַג אֶת בְּכוֹרֵיהֶם, דַּיֵּנוּ.

אִלּוּ הָרַג אֶת בְּכוֹרֵיהֶם וְלֹא נָתַן לָנוּ אֶת מָמוֹנָם, דַּיֵּנוּ.

אִלּוּ נָתַן לָנוּ אֶת מָמוֹנָם וְלֹא קָרַע לָנוּ אֶת הַיָּם, דַּיֵּנוּ.

אִלּוּ קָרַע לָנוּ אֶת הַיָּם וְלֹא הֶעֱבִירָנוּ בְתוֹכוֹ בֶּחָרָבָה, דַּיֵּנוּ.

אִלּוּ הֶעֱבִירָנוּ בְתוֹכוֹ בֶּחָרָבָה וְלֹא שִׁקַּע צָרֵינוּ בְּתוֹכוֹ, דַּיֵּנוּ.

אִלּוּ שִׁקַּע צָרֵינוּ בְּתוֹכוֹ וְלֹא סִפֵּק צָרְכֵּנוּ בַּמִּדְבָּר אַרְבָּעִים שָׁנָה, דַּיֵּנוּ.

אִלּוּ סִפֵּק צָרְכֵּנוּ בַּמִּדְבָּר אַרְבָּעִים שָׁנָה וְלֹא הֶאֱכִילָנוּ אֶת הַמָּן, דַּיֵּנוּ.

אִלּוּ הֶאֱכִילָנוּ אֶת הַמָּן וְלֹא נָתַן לָנוּ אֶת הַשַּׁבָּת, דַּיֵּנוּ.

אִלּוּ נָתַן לָנוּ אֶת הַשַּׁבָּת וְלֹא קֵרְבָנוּ לִפְנֵי הַר סִינַי, דַּיֵּנוּ.

אִלּוּ קֵרְבָנוּ לִפְנֵי הַר סִינַי וְלֹא נָתַן לָנוּ אֶת הַתּוֹרָה, דַּיֵּנוּ.

אִלּוּ נָתַן לָנוּ אֶת הַתּוֹרָה וְלֹא הִכְנִיסָנוּ לְאֶרֶץ יִשְׂרָאֵל, דַּיֵּנוּ.

אִלּוּ הִכְנִיסָנוּ לְאֶרֶץ יִשְׂרָאֵל וְלֹא בָנָה לָנוּ אֶת בֵּית הַבְּחִירָה, דַּיֵּנוּ.

עַל אַחַת כַּמָּה וְכַמָּה טוֹבָה כְפוּלָה וּמְכֻפֶּלֶת לַמָּקוֹם עָלֵינוּ. שֶׁהוֹצִיאָנוּ מִמִּצְרַיִם, וְעָשָׂה בָהֶם שְׁפָטִים, וְעָשָׂה בֵאלֹהֵיהֶם, וְהָרַג אֶת בְּכוֹרֵיהֶם, וְנָתַן לָנוּ אֶת מָמוֹנָם, וְקָרַע לָנוּ אֶת הַיָּם, וְהֶעֱבִירָנוּ בְתוֹכוֹ בֶּחָרָבָה, וְשִׁקַּע צָרֵינוּ בְּתוֹכוֹ, וְסִפֵּק צָרְכֵּנוּ בַּמִּדְבָּר אַרְבָּעִים שָׁנָה, וְהֶאֱכִילָנוּ אֶת הַמָּן, וְנָתַן לָנוּ אֶת הַשַּׁבָּת, וְקֵרְבָנוּ לִפְנֵי הַר סִינַי, וְנָתַן לָנוּ אֶת הַתּוֹרָה, וְהִכְנִיסָנוּ לְאֶרֶץ יִשְׂרָאֵל, וּבָנָה לָנוּ אֶת בֵּית הַבְּחִירָה, לְכַפֵּר עַל כָּל עֲוֹנוֹתֵינוּ.

How much more so have we been shown favor—doubled and redoubled from the On High upon us. That he took us out of Egypt, and delivered judgments against them, and vanquished their gods, and slew their firstborn, and gave us their possessions, and tore the sea in two, and shepherded us through on an arid path, and drowned our tormentors within, and fulfilled our needs for forty years in the desert, and fed us mana, and bequeathed the Shabbat to us, and drew us close to the foot of Mount Sinai, and gave us the Torah, and gathered us into the land of Israel, and built us the Temple for the atonement of all our sins.

The rabbinic scholar Hayim Azulai is born in Jerusalem. At 29, he becomes a shaliach—an emissary to the Diaspora—and travels to Italy to raise money for the Jewish community in Palestine. His work takes him from Amsterdam to Morocco to Warsaw to the West Indies. He then moves to Egypt, where he becomes a rabbi in Cairo. Driven out by a famine, he returns to Palestine and becomes a shaliach again, making his way through Tunisia, France, and the Netherlands before settling in Livorno until his death in 1806. In 1960, his remains are reburied in Jerusalem.

Had He taken us out from Egypt
without delivering judgments against them,   it would have been enough.
Had He delivered judgments against them
without vanquishing their gods,   it would have been enough.
Had He vanquished their gods
without slaying their firstborn,   it would have been enough.
Had He slain their firstborn
without giving us their possessions,   it would have been enough.
Had He given us their possessions
without tearing the sea in two,   it would have been enough.
Had He torn the sea in two
without sheperding us through on an arid path,   it would have been enough.
Had He shepherded us through on an arid path
without drowning our tormentors within,   it would have been enough.
Had He not drowned our tormentors within
without fulfilling our needs for forty years in the desert,   it would have been enough.
Had He not fulfilled our needs for forty years in the
desert without feeding us mana,   it would have been enough.
Had He fed us mana
without bequeathing the Shabbat to us,   it would have been enough.
Had He bequeathed the Shabbat to us
without drawing us close to the foot of Mount Sinai,   it would have been enough.
Had He drawn us close to the foot of Mount Sinai
without giving us the Torah,   it would have been enough.
Had He given us the Torah
without gathering us into the land of Israel,   it would have been enough.
Had He gathered us into the land of Israel
without building the Temple for us,   it would have been enough.

רַבָּן גַּמְלִיאֵל הָיָה אוֹמֵר:
כָּל שֶׁלֹּא אָמַר שְׁלֹשָׁה דְּבָרִים אֵלּוּ
בַּפֶּסַח לֹא יָצָא יְדֵי חוֹבָתוֹ, וְאֵלּוּ הֵן:
פֶּסַח מַצָּה וּמָרוֹר

On April 4, Handel's
oratorio *Israel in
Egypt* premieres
at London's King's
Theater, setting the
"Song at the Sea" to
a new kind of music.

The Continental
Congress creates
a committee to
design a seal for
the new country of
the United States.
Benjamin Franklin
proposes an image
of Pharaoh's chariots
tossed into the sea,
with God's pillar of
flame above and the
words "Rebellion to
Tyrants Is Obedience
to God" below.
Thomas Jefferson's
proposal features
the Israelites in the
wilderness, led by
a cloud of smoke by
day and a pillar of
fire by night.

R abban Gamliel would say: Whoever does not state these
three things on Passover does not fulfill his obligation:
PESACH, MATZAH, and **MAROR.**

Ezekiel Landau, chief
rabbi of Prague, gives
a Passover Shabbat
sermon admonishing
his congregation to
follow the "warning"
of the Haggadah "not
to become insolent
and arrogant," for
"we are only guests.
Even if there should
be a gracious and
compassionate king
who abundantly
helps us, we should
inwardly know that
we are in a land not
our own, and that
we should remain
submissive to the
peoples of that land."

פֶּסַח שֶׁהָיוּ אֲבוֹתֵינוּ אוֹכְלִים בִּזְמַן שֶׁבֵּית הַמִּקְדָּשׁ הָיָה קַיָּם, עַל שׁוּם

מָה? עַל שׁוּם שֶׁפָּסַח הַקָּדוֹשׁ בָּרוּךְ הוּא עַל בָּתֵּי אֲבוֹתֵינוּ בְּמִצְרַיִם, שֶׁנֶּאֱמַר: וַאֲמַרְתֶּם

זֶבַח פֶּסַח הוּא לַיהוה, אֲשֶׁר פָּסַח עַל בָּתֵּי בְנֵי יִשְׂרָאֵל בְּמִצְרַיִם,

בְּנָגְפּוֹ אֶת מִצְרַיִם, וְאֶת בָּתֵּינוּ הִצִּיל, וַיִּקֹּד הָעָם וַיִּשְׁתַּחֲווּ.

מַצָּה זוֹ שֶׁאָנוּ אוֹכְלִים, עַל שׁוּם מָה? עַל שׁוּם שֶׁלֹּא הִסְפִּיק בְּצֵקָם שֶׁל

אֲבוֹתֵינוּ לְהַחֲמִיץ, עַד שֶׁנִּגְלָה עֲלֵיהֶם מֶלֶךְ מַלְכֵי הַמְּלָכִים הַקָּדוֹשׁ בָּרוּךְ הוּא וּגְאָלָם, שֶׁנֶּאֱמַר:

וַיֹּאפוּ אֶת הַבָּצֵק אֲשֶׁר הוֹצִיאוּ מִמִּצְרַיִם עֻגֹת מַצּוֹת, כִּי לֹא חָמֵץ,

כִּי גֹרְשׁוּ מִמִּצְרַיִם וְלֹא יָכְלוּ לְהִתְמַהְמֵהַּ, וְגַם צֵדָה לֹא עָשׂוּ לָהֶם.

מָרוֹר זֶה שֶׁאָנוּ אוֹכְלִים, עַל שׁוּם מָה? עַל שׁוּם שֶׁמֵּרְרוּ הַמִּצְרִים אֶת חַיֵּי

אֲבוֹתֵינוּ בְּמִצְרַיִם, שֶׁנֶּאֱמַר: וַיְמָרְרוּ אֶת חַיֵּיהֶם בַּעֲבֹדָה קָשָׁה, בְּחֹמֶר

וּבִלְבֵנִים וּבְכָל עֲבֹדָה בַּשָּׂדֶה, אֵת כָּל עֲבֹדָתָם אֲשֶׁר עָבְדוּ בָהֶם בְּפָרֶךְ.

On March 3, the Rev.
William White, first
Episcopal bishop of
Pennsylvania and
chaplain to Congress,
uses his visit to the
Orphan Society
of Philadelphia
to deliver an
appropriately themed
sermon: "On the
Drawing of Moses
Out of the Waters."

The "blood libel"—
the accusation of
Jewish ritual murder
of a Christian during
Passover—makes
its first recorded
appearance in
Russia. The accused
are released by local
authorities.

P esach, why did our fathers eat the Passover sacrifice during the era when the Holy Temple still stood? Because the Holy One, Blessed is He, passed over the houses of our fathers in Egypt, as it is written: *And you will say, the slaughtered Passover offering is for the Lord, who passed over the houses of the children of Israel in Egypt, while plaguing Egypt, keeping our houses safe. And the Nation bowed, and lay prone.*

Raise the middle (broken) matzah and say:

M atzah, why do we eat this one? Because the dough of our fathers didn't manage to leaven before the Holy One, Blessed is He, the King of the Heavenly Kings of All Kings, was revealed to them, and redeemed them, as it is written: *And they baked the dough that they took out of Egypt into cakes of matzah, for it had not leavened; for they were driven from Egypt, unable to linger, and also, they had not prepared provisions for themselves.*

Put the matzah back. Raise the maror and say:

M aror, why are we eating this bitter herb? Because the Egyptians embittered the lives of our fathers in Egypt, as it is written: *And they embittered their lives with hard work, with clay and with bricks and all the labor in the fields; all the toil imposed upon them was with a vigor that wore at their bones.*

Put the maror down and continue:

Rossini's opera *Moses in Egypt* is a hit throughout Europe. The melody for Moses' prayer for delivery from slavery becomes a recurring source of inspiration for variations and arrangements throughout the 19th century.

In response to the growing popularity of the American temperance movement, Mordecai Noah, publisher of the *New York Evening Star* and founder of Ararat, a failed homeland for the Jews in upstate New York, publishes a guide to making what he calls temperance wine, a recipe for unfermented raisin wine used by New York's Sephardic Jews for Passover.

בְּכָל דּוֹר וָדוֹר חַיָּב אָדָם לִרְאוֹת אֶת עַצְמוֹ כְּאִלּוּ הוּא יָצָא מִמִּצְרַיִם, שֶׁנֶּאֱמַר: וְהִגַּדְתָּ לְבִנְךָ בַּיּוֹם הַהוּא לֵאמֹר: בַּעֲבוּר זֶה עָשָׂה יהוה לִי בְּצֵאתִי מִמִּצְרָיִם. לֹא אֶת אֲבוֹתֵינוּ בִּלְבָד גָּאַל הַקָּדוֹשׁ בָּרוּךְ הוּא, אֶלָּא אַף אוֹתָנוּ גָּאַל עִמָּהֶם, שֶׁנֶּאֱמַר: וְאוֹתָנוּ הוֹצִיא מִשָּׁם לְמַעַן הָבִיא אֹתָנוּ לָתֶת לָנוּ אֶת הָאָרֶץ אֲשֶׁר נִשְׁבַּע לַאֲבֹתֵינוּ.

I n every generation, a person is obligated to view himself as if he were the one who went out from Egypt, as it is said: *And on that day tell your son, saying, "For this purpose the Lord labored on my behalf, by taking me out of Egypt."* It was not our fathers alone who were delivered by the Holy One, Blessed is He—we were also delivered with them, as it is said: *And He took us out from there in order to bring us—to give us! —the land that He pledged to our fathers.*

Haggadah means narration, and tonight's celebration insists on the moral seriousness of the stories that we tell about ourselves. Stories are easily dismissible as distractions, the make-believe we craved as children, losing ourselves in the sweet enchantment of "as if." "As if" belongs to the imagination, that wild terrain governed by no obvious rules. But tonight we are asked to take this faculty of the mind, so beloved by children and novelists, extremely seriously. All the adults who have outgrown story time are to be tutored tonight, with the physical props meant to quicken our pretending, and the ways of the child to guide us.

It is not enough to merely tell the story, but we must live inside of it, blur the boundaries of our personal narrative so that we spill outward and include as part of our formative experiences having lived through events that took place millennia before we were born.

It is the imagination alone that can extend the sense of the self, broaden our sense of who we really are. We are Jews, insists the tradition, and the identity of an individual Jew is never strictly individual but also collective. By extending our personal narratives to include the formative tale of Jewish identity we appropriate that collective self as part of our own.

But the tradition also insists on possessing tonight's story in more general moral terms, the Torah reminding us never to oppress the stranger, "since you know the soul of the stranger, having been strangers in the land of Egypt." This story that we relive tonight is meant to grant us knowledge of "the soul of the stranger," and there is nothing more universal than that soul and our knowledge of it, and it is only the tutored imagination that can lead us to it and to the compassion it yields.

Tonight is the night that we sanctify storytelling.

Library

Who can say we've actually left? "Wherever you live, it is probably Egypt," Michael Walzer wrote.

Do you live in a place where some people work two and three jobs to feed their children, and others don't even have a single, poorly paid job? Do you live in a community in which the rich are fabulously rich, and the poor humiliated and desperate? Do you live among people who worship the golden calves of obsessive acquisitiveness, among people whose children are blessed by material abundance and cursed by spiritual impoverishment? Do you live in a place in which some people are more equal than others?

In America, the unemployment rate for African-Americans is nearly twice as high as it is for whites. Black people are five times as likely to be incarcerated as whites. Infant mortality in the black community is twice as high as it is among whites. America is a golden land, absolutely, and for Jews, it has been an ark of refuge. But it has not yet fulfilled its promise. The same is true for that other Promised Land. Jewish citizens of Israel have median household incomes almost double that of Arab citizens and an infant mortality rate less than half that of Arabs. Israel represents the greatest miracle in Jewish life in two thousand years—and its achievements are stupendous (and not merely in comparison to its dysfunctional neighbors)— and yet its promise is also unfulfilled. The seder marks the flight from the humiliation of slavery to the grandeur of freedom, but not everyone has come on this journey. It is impossible to love the stranger as much as we love our own kin, but aren't we still commanded to bring everyone out of Egypt?

Nation

"In every generation

each person must look upon himself as if he left Egypt."

House of Study

In Exodus 12, God invents the holiday of Passover when he commands Moses and Aaron to tell "the whole community of

Israel": "Seven days you shall eat unleavened bread....You shall observe the [Feast of] Unleavened Bread, for on this very day I brought your ranks out of the land of Egypt; you shall observe this day throughout the ages as an institution for all time." (Exodus 12:15) In the following chapter, Moses relays God's command, declaring: "Seven days you shall eat unleavened bread, and on the seventh day there shall be a festival of the Lord." (Exodus 13:6)

But there is a crucial difference.

Where God uses the plural form of "you" in the Hebrew original, Moses substitutes the singular form; where God directs his command to the entire nation, Moses redirects it to the individual Israelite, adding "And you shall explain to your son on that day, 'It is because of what the LORD did for me when I went free from Egypt.'" (Exodus 13:8)

The "whole community of Israel" has now become "your son," and "your ranks" have become "me."

In many places, the Torah teaches us that Jews were chosen as individuals? Perhaps in order that the collective should not eclipse or even erase our individual selves, the Haggadah reminds us that every "person is obligated to view himself as if he were the one who went out from Egypt." In this way, we continue to fulfill Moses' exhortation to tell our children about what the "Lord did for me when I left Egypt"—for me and not for you or, even, for us.

But do we still need to be reminded that we are individuals? Or is the real challenge to imagine that we belong to something bigger than ourselves?

Playground

The story of Passover may seem very remote to you, as it happened thousands of years ago, when the

oldest people at your seder table were very, very young, and so many of the details of the story seem somewhat old-fashioned, such as the smearing of lamb's blood over the doorway of one's home, which has largely been replaced by signs warning away solicitors. But in fact, the story of liberation is one that is still going on, as people all over the world are still in bondage, and we wait and wait, as the Jews in Egypt waited and waited, for the day when freedom will be spread all over the world like frosting on a well-made cake, rather than dabbed on here and there as if the baker were selfishly eating most of the frosting directly from the bowl. The story of Passover is a journey, and like most journeys, it is taking much longer than it ought to take, no matter how many times we stop and ask for directions. We must look upon ourselves as though we, too, were among those fleeing a life of bondage in Egypt and wandering the desert for years and years, which is why we are often so tired in the evenings and cannot always explain how we got to be exactly where we are.

In his novel *The Rabbi of Bacharach*, the German writer and convert from Judaism Heinrich Heine describes Passover as a festival "melancholically gay in character, gravely playful, and mysterious as a fairy tale. And the traditional singsong in which the Haggadah is read... sounds at the same time so awesomely intense, maternally gentle, and suddenly awakening, that even those Jews who have long forsaken the faith of their fathers and pursued foreign joys and honors are moved to the depths of their hearts when the old, familiar sounds of the Passover happen to strike their ears."

לְפִיכָךְ, אֲנַחְנוּ חַיָּבִים לְהוֹדוֹת, לְהַלֵּל, לְשַׁבֵּחַ, לְפָאֵר, לְרוֹמֵם, לְהַדֵּר, לְבָרֵךְ, לְעַלֵּה וּלְקַלֵּס לְמִי שֶׁעָשָׂה לַאֲבוֹתֵינוּ וְלָנוּ אֶת כָּל הַנִּסִּים הָאֵלּוּ. הוֹצִיאָנוּ מֵעַבְדוּת לְחֵרוּת, מִיָּגוֹן לְשִׂמְחָה, מֵאֵבֶל לְיוֹם טוֹב, וּמֵאֲפֵלָה לְאוֹר גָּדוֹל, וּמִשִּׁעְבּוּד לִגְאֻלָּה, וְנֹאמַר לְפָנָיו שִׁירָה חֲדָשָׁה, הַלְלוּיָהּ.

הַלְלוּיָהּ, הַלְלוּ עַבְדֵי יהוה
הַלְלוּ אֶת שֵׁם יהוה.
יְהִי שֵׁם יהוה מְבֹרָךְ
מֵעַתָּה וְעַד עוֹלָם.
מִמִּזְרַח שֶׁמֶשׁ עַד מְבוֹאוֹ
מְהֻלָּל שֵׁם יהוה.
רָם עַל כָּל גּוֹיִם יהוה
עַל הַשָּׁמַיִם כְּבוֹדוֹ.
מִי כַּיהוה אֱלֹהֵינוּ
הַמַּגְבִּיהִי לָשָׁבֶת.
הַמַּשְׁפִּילִי לִרְאוֹת
בַּשָּׁמַיִם וּבָאָרֶץ.
מְקִימִי מֵעָפָר דָּל
מֵאַשְׁפֹּת יָרִים אֶבְיוֹן.
לְהוֹשִׁיבִי עִם נְדִיבִים
עִם נְדִיבֵי עַמּוֹ.
מוֹשִׁיבִי עֲקֶרֶת הַבַּיִת
אֵם הַבָּנִים שְׂמֵחָה.
הַלְלוּיָהּ.

1857

The first matzah
baking machine is
invented in Austria,
sparking decades
of debate over
whether machine-
made matzah can
be kosher.

1840

In response to
the blood libel
against the Jews
of Damascus in
February, the
August 17 edition
of the London
Times features a full
English translation
of the Haggadah to
demonstrate that the
Passover ritual in no
way involves the use
of Christian blood.

*Cover the
matzot, raise the
cup, and say:*

Hence, we are obligated to give thanks, to sing praise, to venerate, to glorify, to exalt, to beautify, to bless, to uplift and applaud the One who performed all these miracles for our fathers and for us. He brought us from slavery to freedom, from sorrow to joy, from grief to good days, from gloom to great radiance, from servitude to redemption, and we recite before Him a new song, *Hallelujah*.

*Put down the
cup, uncover
the matzot, and
continue:*

Hallelujah: sing praises, servants of the Lord,
sing praises of the Lord's name!
May the name of the Lord be blessed,
        now and forever.
From the sun's eastern rise and on to its westering
        be praised the name of the Lord.
Poised above all other nations is the Lord,
        over the heavens rests His honor.
Who is like the Lord God-of-Us,
        enthroned on high,
Inclining to gaze in
        upon the heavens and upon the earth.
He raises up the impoverished from dust,
        from rubbish heaps, He lifts the poor,
To seat them with princes,
        among the noblemen of His realm.
He restores the barren of the house,
        and a mother with children rejoices:
           Hallelujah!

In *Mozes*, the
Hungarian playwright
Imre Madách uses
the Exodus story
as a parable for
Hungary's struggle for
independence from
the Hapsburg Empire.

While camped
with the 23rd Ohio
Volunteer Regiment
of the Union army in
West Virginia, Joseph
Joel and fellow
soldiers prepare for
Passover by foraging
in the woods for
chickens, eggs, a
lamb, and weeds to
use as bitter herbs.
The weeds prove
so bitter that the
celebrants drink
far more than the
specified four cups of
alcohol, and two men
claiming to be Moses
and Pharaoh get into
a drunken brawl.

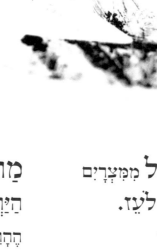

מַה לְּךָ הַיָּם כִּי תָנוּס
הַיַּרְדֵּן תִּסֹּב לְאָחוֹר.
הֶהָרִים תִּרְקְדוּ כְאֵילִים
גְּבָעוֹת כִּבְנֵי צֹאן.
מִלִּפְנֵי אָדוֹן חוּלִי אָרֶץ
מִלִּפְנֵי אֱלוֹהַּ יַעֲקֹב.
הַהֹפְכִי הַצּוּר אֲגַם מָיִם
חַלָּמִישׁ לְמַעְיְנוֹ מָיִם.

בְּצֵאת יִשְׂרָאֵל מִמִּצְרָיִם
בֵּית יַעֲקֹב מֵעַם לֹעֵז.
הָיְתָה יְהוּדָה לְקָדְשׁוֹ
יִשְׂרָאֵל מַמְשְׁלוֹתָיו.
הַיָּם רָאָה וַיָּנֹס
הַיַּרְדֵּן יִסֹּב לְאָחוֹר.
הֶהָרִים רָקְדוּ כְאֵילִים
גְּבָעוֹת כִּבְנֵי צֹאן.

Jacob and Aaron
David Talkar publish
a Haggadah in the
Indian language of
Marathi featuring
illustrations of
men and women in
traditional Indian
dress. The Haggadah
is for India's Bene
Israel—Arabic-
speaking Jews who,
legend has it, were
shipwrecked on the
Konkan coast two
millennia earlier.

With the Exodus of Israel from Egypt,
      the House of Jacob emerged from a foreign nation.
      Judah became His sanctuary,
    Israel His dominion.
The sea saw this and fled,
      the Jordan turned back.
The mountains danced, skipping like rams,
      the heights like lambs.
What has happened to you, the Sea, that you are now fleeing,
      the Jordan, that you are turning back?
The Mountains, that you dance, skipping like rams,
      and the Heights, like lambs?
From facing the Master who unfurled the earth,
      from facing Jacob's God,
The One who turns rock into reservoir,
      flint into freshwater spring.

Chaim Weizmann, scientist and first president of the State of Israel, is born in Motol, Belorussia. At 11, Weizmann moves to Pinsk, the provincial capital, for school. He continues his studies in Darmstadt, Berlin, and Fribourg, Switzerland, and after finishing his thesis takes a teaching post in Geneva. In 1904, he moves to Manchester to continue his academic career before moving in 1937 to Israel, where he ends his wanderings, settling in Rehovot until his death in 1952.

In San Francisco, the social reformer Henry George delivers a speech on Moses as the model emancipator whose rejection of God's offer to replace the stubborn band of Israelites with a new Chosen People demonstrates the value of solidarity.

בָּרוּךְ אַתָּה יהוה, אֱלֹהֵינוּ מֶלֶךְ הָעוֹלָם, אֲשֶׁר גְּאָלָנוּ וְגָאַל אֶת אֲבוֹתֵינוּ מִמִּצְרַיִם, וְהִגִּיעָנוּ הַלַּיְלָה הַזֶּה לֶאֱכָל בּוֹ מַצָּה וּמָרוֹר. כֵּן יהוה אֱלֹהֵינוּ וֵאלֹהֵי אֲבוֹתֵינוּ, יַגִּיעֵנוּ לְמוֹעֲדִים וְלִרְגָלִים אֲחֵרִים הַבָּאִים לִקְרָאתֵנוּ לְשָׁלוֹם, שְׂמֵחִים בְּבִנְיַן עִירֶךָ, וְשָׂשִׂים בַּעֲבוֹדָתֶךָ, וְנֹאכַל שָׁם מִן הַזְּבָחִים וּמִן הַפְּסָחִים [במוצאי שבת מחליפים: מִן הַפְּסָחִים וּמִן הַזְּבָחִים] אֲשֶׁר יַגִּיעַ דָּמָם עַל קִיר מִזְבַּחֲךָ לְרָצוֹן, וְנוֹדֶה לְךָ שִׁיר חָדָשׁ עַל גְּאֻלָּתֵנוּ וְעַל פְּדוּת נַפְשֵׁנוּ. בָּרוּךְ אַתָּה יהוה גָּאַל יִשְׂרָאֵל.

In a visual commentary on the throngs of immigrants making their way from Europe to the United States, the satiric British magazine *Puck* publishes a cartoon showing Uncle Sam, swathed in biblical garb, as a modern Moses parting the waters of "intolerance" and "oppression" to make way for an endless procession of caricatured Jews, from poor villagers with their belongings on their back to rich bankers with stovepipe hats and monocles.

Cover the matzot, raise the cup, and continue:

Y ou are blessed, Lord God-of-Us, King of the Cosmos, who delivered us, and delivered our fathers, from Egypt, who brought us to this night, to eat in its course matzah and maror. So, too, may You — Lord God-of-Us and God of our fathers — bear us through to the holidays and festivals, heading to meet us in peace, when we will be joyous in rebuilding Your city and rejoicing in Your worship, where we will eat from the slaughtered offerings and from the Pascal sacrifices [on Saturday nights, reverse the order to: "from the Pascal sacrifices and from the slaughtered offerings"] whose blood shall run down the wall of Your altar as is Your desire. And we acknowledge You with new song, singing of our liberation and the loosing of our souls. You are blessed, Lord, He who delivered forth Israel.

Second Cup כּוֹס שֵׁנִי

H ere I am, prepared and ardent, allied and present, ready to perform the mitzvah of the second cup, the enactment of salvation's promise. As the Holy One, Blessed is He, declared to Israel: *And I will rescue you from your enslavement.*

הִנְנִי מוּכָן/מוּכָנָה וּמְזֻמָּן/וּמְזֻמֶּנֶת לְקַיֵּם מִצְוַת כּוֹס שֵׁנִי שֶׁהוּא כְּנֶגֶד בְּשׂוֹרַת הַיְשׁוּעָה שֶׁאָמַר הַקָּדוֹשׁ בָּרוּךְ הוּא לְיִשְׂרָאֵל: וְהִצַּלְתִּי אֶתְכֶם מֵעֲבֹדָתָם.

You are blessed, Lord God-of-Us, King of the Cosmos, Maker of the fruit of the vine.

בָּרוּךְ אַתָּה יהוה, אֱלֹהֵינוּ מֶלֶךְ הָעוֹלָם, בּוֹרֵא פְּרִי הַגָּפֶן.

While reclining, drink at least most of the cup of wine.

1882

Inspired by the Zionist movements of Bilu and Hibbat Zion, the first large-scale migration to Israel in modern Jewish history begins with the "First Aliyah" of 25,000 Jews, primarily from Eastern Europe.

רָחְצָה

בָּרוּךְ אַתָּה יהוה, אֱלֹהֵינוּ מֶלֶךְ הָעוֹלָם, אֲשֶׁר קִדְּשָׁנוּ בְּמִצְוֹתָיו, וְצִוָּנוּ עַל נְטִילַת יָדָיִם.

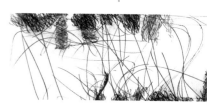

מוֹצִיא

בָּרוּךְ אַתָּה יהוה, אֱלֹהֵינוּ מֶלֶךְ הָעוֹלָם, הַמּוֹצִיא לֶחֶם מִן הָאָרֶץ.

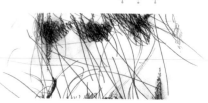

מַצָּה

בָּרוּךְ אַתָּה יהוה, אֱלֹהֵינוּ מֶלֶךְ הָעוֹלָם, אֲשֶׁר קִדְּשָׁנוּ בְּמִצְוֹתָיו, וְצִוָּנוּ עַל אֲכִילַת מַצָּה.

מָרוֹר

בָּרוּךְ אַתָּה יהוה, אֱלֹהֵינוּ מֶלֶךְ הָעוֹלָם, אֲשֶׁר קִדְּשָׁנוּ בְּמִצְוֹתָיו, וְצִוָּנוּ עַל אֲכִילַת מָרוֹר.

The future anarchist and activist Emma Goldman arrives in New York City. Born in Kovno, she moves with her family to Königsberg and then St. Petersburg before setting out for the United States at 16. She launches her career as an advocate for workers' rights and women's liberation, but after the United States enters World War I she is designated a threat to national security and is deported. She returns to Russia, but is disillusioned by the increasingly anti-democratic Soviet regime and drifts between England, France, and Canada before her death in Toronto in 1940.

Rahtza

Wash your hands fully and recite:

You are blessed, Lord God-of-Us, King of the Cosmos, who has set us apart with his mitzvot, and instructed us regarding the washing of the hands.

Dry your hands and refrain from talking until after eating the matzah.

Motzi

Raise the three matzot and recite:

You are blessed, Lord God-of-Us, King of the Cosmos, who draws forth bread from the land.

Matzah

Put the bottom matzah back on the plate and, while continuing to hold the top two, recite (keeping in mind that this blessing also applies to the matzah to be eaten later):

You are blessed, Lord God-of-Us, King of the Cosmos, who has set us apart with his mitzvot, and instructed us regarding the eating of matzah.

While reclining to the left, quickly eat a generous portion of each of the two top matzot.

Maror

Take some of the maror vegetable, dip into the charoset, and recite (keeping in mind that this blessing also applies to the korech):

You are blessed, Lord God-of-Us, King of the Cosmos, who has set us apart with his mitzvot, and instructed us regarding the eating of maror.

Quickly eat it without reclining.

In an autobiographical essay in the London *Jewish Chronicle*, Theodor Herzl, the founder of the Zionist movement, writes of his childhood in Budapest: "I was sent to a Jewish preparatory school, where I enjoyed a certain authority because my father was a wealthy merchant. My earliest recollection of the school consists of a caning which I received from the master because I didn't know the details of the exodus of the Jews from Egypt. At the present time a great many schoolmasters want to give me a caning, because I recollect too much of the exodus from Egypt."

כּוֹרֵךְ

זֵכֶר לְמִקְדָּשׁ כְּהִלֵּל. כֵּן עָשָׂה הִלֵּל בִּזְמַן שֶׁבֵּית הַמִּקְדָּשׁ הָיָה קַיָם. הָיָה **כּוֹרֵךְ מַצָּה וּמָרוֹר** וְאוֹכֵל בְּיַחַד, לְקַיֵם מַה שֶׁנֶּאֱמַר: עַל מַצּוֹת וּמְרֹרִים יֹאכְלֻהוּ.

שֻׁלְחָן עוֹרֵךְ

צָפוּן

בָּרֵךְ

שִׁיר הַמַּעֲלוֹת. בְּשׁוּב יהוה אֶת שִׁיבַת צִיּוֹן הָיִינוּ כְּחֹלְמִים. אָז יִמָּלֵא שְׂחוֹק פִּינוּ וּלְשׁוֹנֵנוּ רִנָּה. אָז יֹאמְרוּ בַגּוֹיִם הִגְדִּיל יהוה לַעֲשׂוֹת עִם אֵלֶּה. הִגְדִּיל יהוה לַעֲשׂוֹת עִמָּנוּ, הָיִינוּ שְׂמֵחִים. שׁוּבָה יהוה אֶת שְׁבִיתֵנוּ כַּאֲפִיקִים בַּנֶּגֶב. הַזֹּרְעִים בְּדִמְעָה בְּרִנָּה יִקְצֹרוּ. הָלוֹךְ יֵלֵךְ וּבָכֹה, נֹשֵׂא מֶשֶׁךְ הַזָּרַע, בֹּא יָבֹא בְרִנָּה, נֹשֵׂא אֲלֻמֹּתָיו.

1898

In his landmark book, *The Interpretation of Dreams*, Sigmund Freud recounts his dream—known in psychoanalytic history as "My Son, the Myopic"—in which his eldest son utters the nonsense phrase "auf Ungeseres." Freud interprets this as a reference to *ungesauertes Brot*, unleavened bread, evoking the flight from Egypt and making the dream a parable of escape.

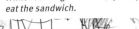

Korech

Make a sandwich from some of the bottom matzah and some more maror, dip in the charoset, and say:

A commemoration of the Temple, in the style of Hillel. During the epoch in which the Holy Temple was standing, Hillel performed it in this manner: He would bundle Pascal meat, matzah, and maror and eat them together to fulfill what is written: *With matzot and maror, they shall eat it.*

While reclining to the left, quickly eat the sandwich.

Shulhan Oreh

Some begin the meal with a hard-boiled egg dipped in salt water.

Tzafun

Once the meal is finished, the children retrieve the afikoman (demanding a reward once it has been found). Eat it while reclining to the left. Once the afikoman has been eaten, refrain from eating for the rest of the night.

Bareh

Refill the wine cup and recite:

A Song of Ascents. When the Lord returns us—the repatriated of Zion—we will be as if dreamers. It is then that our mouths will swell with laughter, our tongues be overspread with songs of joy. It is then they will exclaim among nations: "Magnificent is what the Lord has done for them." And magnificent is what the Lord has done for us, we were exultant. Return, Lord, our captives, sure as the wadis will course the Negev. For those that sow with tears, with joy will reap. Walks on the walker crying, bearing the sack of seed; then comes the comer, rejoicing, carrying his sheaves.

God enters history. Israel becomes a nation. The Torah is given at Sinai. Exodus overflows with revelations.

And yet, the story of the Exodus from Egypt begins with a small and poignant act of concealment: "A certain man of the house of Levi went and married a Levite woman. The woman conceived and bore a son; and when she saw how beautiful he was, she hid him for three months. When she could hide him no longer, she got a wicker basket…put the child into it and placed it among the reeds by the bank of the Nile. And his sister stationed herself at a distance, to learn what would befall him."

Separated from his family and his people, that beautiful boy would be discovered, crying, by the daughter of Pharaoh, who "took pity on him." She would give him the name Moses and raise him as her own son.

Concealed yet again, this time as an Egyptian prince, Moses would later be revealed as an Israelite prophet of whom Deuteronomy declares: "Never again did there arise in Israel a prophet like Moses—whom the Lord singled out, face to face."

House of Study

Like the Exodus from Egypt, the drama of the seder is set into motion by an act of concealment: the hiding of the afikoman, a piece broken off from the middle matzah symbolizing the Levites, the tribe to which that beautiful boy belonged. During the course of the seder, we relive the world-shattering revelations of Exodus, but always, in the back of our minds, like Miriam stationed at a distance, we remember that something essential remains concealed, waiting to be discovered.

Isaac Luria, the great Kabbalist known as Ha-Ari (the Lion), taught that in order to create the world, God first contracted into himself, a process known as tsimtsum in Hebrew. This, he explained, was the original act of concealment—of hiding. Without it, there would be no space for atsilut, the divine emanation that is the first stage of creation—of revelation.

The Torah describes Moses as "a very humble man, more so than any other man on earth." (Numbers 12:3) Humility, like contraction, is another form of concealment.

We live in a world in which more is often better; in which so many of us reveal so much. But when is more actually less? When is it important to conceal rather than reveal?

The afikoman is the hostage of the Passover seder, having been ripped from its neighboring matzah, imprisoned in an obscure part of the house, and then traded for some ransom just so it can be split up and devoured. Decent people will not participate in this saga of kidnapping and blackmail but rather fight against these foul crimes by excusing themselves from the meal during the meal to disseminate counterfeit afikomans, a phrase which here means "hiding similar pieces of matzah all over the house." Soon everyone will have found an afikoman, and negotiations will break down in a flurry of accusations and crumbs. Another word for this state of affairs is "freedom."

Playground

Afikoman

At the beginning of the first Palestinian uprising, the Israeli army built an open-air prison called Ketziot, near the border with Egypt.

The prison, which was meant to warehouse Palestinians arrested in Gaza and the West Bank, sat a few miles from the site of Kadesh Barnea, where Moses defied God. Moses was punished for his transgression when God denied him entrance to the Promised Land.

The prison at Ketziot held, at various times, as many as six thousand Palestinians, from the lowliest rock throwers to the leaders of the uprising. Three hundred or so Israeli soldiers made up the staff. The food, for prisoners and soldiers alike, was kosher, because the Israeli army is a kosher army. So at Passover, the prisoners ate only matzah, just as the soldiers did. One Passover day, a leader of the prisoners, a terrorist who had murdered a Jew several years earlier, summoned a soldier to the barbed-wire fence that surrounded the compound. He explained politely, with a good deal of hesitation, that the Palestinian prisoners didn't actually like the taste of matzah. The soldier said, "We don't like it either" and explained the notion of the bread of affliction. "But we're the afflicted!" the prisoner cried out. The soldier said, "You murdered a Jew and you say you're afflicted?" The conversation went nowhere, as these sorts of conversations tend to do. And yet the soldier learned something from the encounter.

A couple of days earlier, at the soldier's seder—a rushed seder under an army tent—the afikoman was broken, signifying, among other things, the shattering pain of enslavement. At the end of the seder, when each participant is meant to eat a piece of the afikoman, thereby completing the journey to the wholeness of freedom, the soldier ate, but with an unsettled feeling. It was, he realized later, a feeling of ongoing affliction that made the afikoman bitter.

The afikoman is a very useful metaphor. A child's literal search for the afikoman symbolizes our own search for wholeness. We have within us a profound desire for harmony, for feeling at one with our fellow men and women. Prisons symbolize the brokenness of the world. And yet we are tragically aware that we need them. The afikoman is a reminder that, for now, the world is unfixed, that it is, in its own way, a prison, in which even the free are captives.

Nation

The seder is an exercise in moral optimism. Look around at all the symbols arranged on the table.

They either remind us of suffering—of tears and of bitterness, and of a God too distant who allows the groans to go on too long—or they speak of a hope-fed future—of spring and of fertility, and of a next year that will see us safe in a Jerusalem of peace.

The afikoman is the symbol that bridges the gap between the tear-stained past and the happier future. It embodies the faith that there is always a way, concealed though it might be, to make the transition from the suffering that we know to the future that we dream. The belief in moral progress is of the essence of the seder's optimism. It is of the essence of a people's faith.

And so we have the ritual of deliberate concealment, of taking the very thing needed to conclude the seder and hiding it, just in order to reveal it at the last possible moment. We make a game of it, for the sake of our children, knowing that we enact in the ritual our deepest faith in their future.

The philosopher Wittgenstein famously wrote, "Of what we cannot speak we must remain silent." All religious rituals, perhaps like all art, are attempts to gesture toward what cannot be spoken, to invoke it and make it palpable, a sense of the world too immense to be summed up in words without sounding like prattling children.

To go through the rituals of the seder, including those four cups of wine, is to feel that, despite our own more sober reflections, a way can be found. We are all in this together, and a way can be found. We will unconceal it, for the sake of our children, as they will unconceal it, for the sake of their children. We sit together with our great diversities of worldviews, for we are celebrants of freedom and will brook no tyranny of thought. But we all eat the afikoman together, gesturing toward a sense of the world that sustains us in our hope.

Library

New York becomes the world's largest Jewish city, a title it will retain for the next century. The city's Jewish population of 598,000, or 17% of the total, is greater than that of the next three largest Jewish cities—Warsaw, Budapest, and London—combined.

רַבּוֹתַי נְבָרֵך

יְהִי שֵׁם יהוה מְבֹרָךְ מֵעַתָּה וְעַד עוֹלָם.

יְהִי שֵׁם יהוה מְבֹרָךְ מֵעַתָּה וְעַד עוֹלָם.

בִּרְשׁוּת מָרָנָן וְרַבָּנָן וְרַבּוֹתַי, נְבָרֵךְ (אֱלֹהֵינוּ) שֶׁאָכַלְנוּ מִשֶּׁלוֹ.

בָּרוּךְ (אֱלֹהֵינוּ) שֶׁאָכַלְנוּ מִשֶּׁלוֹ וּבְטוּבוֹ חָיִינוּ.

בָּרוּךְ (אֱלֹהֵינוּ) שֶׁאָכַלְנוּ מִשֶּׁלוֹ וּבְטוּבוֹ חָיִינוּ.

בָּרוּךְ הוּא וּבָרוּךְ שְׁמוֹ.

בָּרוּךְ אַתָּה יהוה

אֱלֹהֵינוּ מֶלֶךְ הָעוֹלָם, הַזָּן אֶת הָעוֹלָם כֻּלּוֹ בְּטוּבוֹ, בְּחֵן בְּחֶסֶד וּבְרַחֲמִים. הוּא נוֹתֵן לֶחֶם לְכָל בָּשָׂר כִּי לְעוֹלָם חַסְדּוֹ. וּבְטוּבוֹ הַגָּדוֹל תָּמִיד לֹא חָסַר לָנוּ וְאַל יֶחְסַר לָנוּ מָזוֹן לְעוֹלָם וָעֶד, בַּעֲבוּר שְׁמוֹ הַגָּדוֹל, כִּי הוּא אֵל זָן וּמְפַרְנֵס לַכֹּל, וּמֵטִיב לַכֹּל וּמֵכִין מָזוֹן לְכָל בְּרִיּוֹתָיו אֲשֶׁר בָּרָא. בָּרוּךְ אַתָּה יהוה, הַזָּן אֶת הַכֹּל.

נוֹדֶה לְךָ יהוה

אֱלֹהֵינוּ עַל שֶׁהִנְחַלְתָּ לַאֲבוֹתֵינוּ אֶרֶץ חֶמְדָּה טוֹבָה וּרְחָבָה, וְעַל שֶׁהוֹצֵאתָנוּ יהוה אֱלֹהֵינוּ מֵאֶרֶץ מִצְרַיִם, וּפְדִיתָנוּ מִבֵּית עֲבָדִים, וְעַל בְּרִיתְךָ שֶׁחָתַמְתָּ בִּבְשָׂרֵנוּ, וְעַל תּוֹרָתְךָ שֶׁלִּמַּדְתָּנוּ, וְעַל חֻקֶּיךָ שֶׁהוֹדַעְתָּנוּ, וְעַל חַיִּים חֵן וָחֶסֶד שֶׁחוֹנַנְתָּנוּ, וְעַל אֲכִילַת מָזוֹן שָׁאַתָּה זָן וּמְפַרְנֵס אוֹתָנוּ תָּמִיד, בְּכָל יוֹם וּבְכָל עֵת וּבְכָל שָׁעָה.

וְעַל הַכֹּל יהוה אֱלֹהֵינוּ אֲנַחְנוּ מוֹדִים לָךְ וּמְבָרְכִים אוֹתָךְ. יִתְבָּרַךְ שִׁמְךָ בְּפִי כָּל חַי תָּמִיד לְעוֹלָם וָעֶד, כַּכָּתוּב: וְאָכַלְתָּ וְשָׂבָעְתָּ וּבֵרַכְתָּ אֶת יהוה אֱלֹהֶיךָ עַל הָאָרֶץ הַטּוֹבָה אֲשֶׁר נָתַן לָךְ. בָּרוּךְ אַתָּה יהוה, עַל הָאָרֶץ וְעַל הַמָּזוֹן.

1905

1904

In Calcutta, India, David Hai Eini commissions a trilingual Haggadah in Hebrew, Arabic, and English to meet the needs of the Bene Israel and Jews who have learned English under the rule of the British Mandate.

The Zionist writer Asher Ginsberg, writing under his pen name of Ahad Ha'Am—Hebrew for "one of the people"—maintains that Moses "has been our leader not only for forty years in the wilderness of Sinai, but for thousands of years in all the wildernesses in which we have wandered since the Exodus."

If there are at least three participants, say the following responsively. (If there are at least ten, include the words in brackets.) If there are fewer than three, skip to "You are blessed..."

Leader:	My teachers, let us bless.
Others:	May the name of the Lord be blessed, now and forever.
Leader:	May the name of the Lord be blessed, now and forever. Gentlefolk, dear masters, my teachers, with your permission, let us bless [our God,] He from whose bounty we have partaken.
Others:	Blessed is [our God,] He from whose bounty we have partaken, and by whose goodness we live.
Leader:	Blessed is [our God,] He from whose bounty we have partaken, and by whose goodness we live.
Everyone:	Blessed is He, and blessed is His name.

You are blessed,

Lord God-of-Us, King of the Cosmos, who nourishes the world in whole through His goodness: with grace, with munificence and compassion. He provides food to all flesh, because His kindness is without end. And in His great goodness, we are never left lacking. He will never leave us wanting for nourishment by virtue of His great name, because He is a God who nourishes and gives sustenance to all, and improves the plight of all, and prepares food for all His creations, created by Him. You are blessed, Lord, who nourishes all.

We thank you,

Lord God-of-Us, for having bequeathed to our fathers a land desirable, rich, and broad; for having taken us out, Lord God-of-Us, from the land of Egypt; for having redeemed us from the house of bondage; for Your covenant that You stamped in our flesh; for Your Torah that You taught us; for Your laws of which You apprised us, and for the life, favor, and kindness with which You graced us; and for the food with which You nourish and sustain us always—through every day, through every era, through every turn.

And for the entirety, Lord God-of-Us, we thank You and we bless You. Let Your name be blessed in the mouth of all life always, eternally and on, as it is written: *After you have eaten and when you are sated, you will bless the Lord your God for the choice land that was given to you.* You are blessed, Lord, for the land and for the sustenance.

On January 8, the Reform leader Kaufmann Kohler gives a speech to the Union of American Hebrew Congregations: "Least of all could Judaism retain its medieval garb, its alien form, its seclusiveness, in a country that rolled off the shame and the taunt of the centuries from the shoulders of the wandering Jew… among a people that adopted the very principles of justice and human dignity proclaimed by Israel's lawgivers and prophets, and made them the foundation stones of their commonwealth."

רַחֵם יהוה אֱלֹהֵינוּ עַל יִשְׂרָאֵל עַמֶּךָ, וְעַל יְרוּשָׁלַיִם עִירֶךָ, וְעַל צִיּוֹן מִשְׁכַּן כְּבוֹדֶךָ, וְעַל מַלְכוּת בֵּית דָּוִד מְשִׁיחֶךָ, וְעַל הַבַּיִת הַגָּדוֹל וְהַקָּדוֹשׁ שֶׁנִּקְרָא שִׁמְךָ עָלָיו. אֱלֹהֵינוּ אָבִינוּ, רְעֵנוּ זוּנֵנוּ, פַּרְנְסֵנוּ וְכַלְכְּלֵנוּ וְהַרְוִיחֵנוּ, וְהַרְוַח לָנוּ יהוה אֱלֹהֵינוּ מְהֵרָה מִכָּל צָרוֹתֵינוּ. וְנָא אַל תַּצְרִיכֵנוּ יהוה אֱלֹהֵינוּ, לֹא לִידֵי מַתְּנַת בָּשָׂר וָדָם וְלֹא לִידֵי הַלְוָאָתָם, כִּי אִם לְיָדְךָ הַמְּלֵאָה הַפְּתוּחָה הַקְּדוֹשָׁה וְהָרְחָבָה, שֶׁלֹּא נֵבוֹשׁ וְלֹא נִכָּלֵם לְעוֹלָם וָעֶד.

רְצֵה וְהַחֲלִיצֵנוּ יהוה אֱלֹהֵינוּ בְּמִצְוֹתֶיךָ, וּבְמִצְוַת יוֹם הַשְּׁבִיעִי הַשַּׁבָּת הַגָּדוֹל וְהַקָּדוֹשׁ הַזֶּה, כִּי יוֹם זֶה גָּדוֹל וְקָדוֹשׁ הוּא לְפָנֶיךָ, לִשְׁבָּת בּוֹ וְלָנוּחַ בּוֹ בְּאַהֲבָה כְּמִצְוַת רְצוֹנֶךָ. וּבִרְצוֹנְךָ הָנִיחַ לָנוּ יהוה אֱלֹהֵינוּ שֶׁלֹּא תְהֵא צָרָה וְיָגוֹן וַאֲנָחָה בְּיוֹם מְנוּחָתֵנוּ. וְהַרְאֵנוּ יהוה אֱלֹהֵינוּ בְּנֶחָמַת צִיּוֹן עִירֶךָ, וּבְבִנְיַן יְרוּשָׁלַיִם עִיר קָדְשֶׁךָ, כִּי אַתָּה הוּא בַּעַל הַיְשׁוּעוֹת וּבַעַל הַנֶּחָמוֹת.

אֱלֹהֵינוּ וֵאלֹהֵי אֲבוֹתֵינוּ, יַעֲלֶה וְיָבֹא, וְיַגִּיעַ וְיֵרָאֶה, וְיֵרָצֶה וְיִשָּׁמַע, וְיִפָּקֵד וְיִזָּכֵר זִכְרוֹנֵנוּ וּפִקְדוֹנֵנוּ, וְזִכְרוֹן אֲבוֹתֵינוּ, וְזִכְרוֹן מָשִׁיחַ בֶּן דָּוִד עַבְדֶּךָ, וְזִכְרוֹן יְרוּשָׁלַיִם עִיר קָדְשֶׁךָ, וְזִכְרוֹן כָּל עַמְּךָ בֵּית יִשְׂרָאֵל לְפָנֶיךָ, לִפְלֵיטָה וּלְטוֹבָה, לְחֵן וּלְחֶסֶד וּלְרַחֲמִים, וּלְחַיִּים וּלְשָׁלוֹם בְּיוֹם חַג הַמַּצּוֹת הַזֶּה. זָכְרֵנוּ יהוה אֱלֹהֵינוּ בּוֹ לְטוֹבָה, וּפָקְדֵנוּ בוֹ לִבְרָכָה, וְהוֹשִׁיעֵנוּ בוֹ לְחַיִּים. וּבִדְבַר יְשׁוּעָה וְרַחֲמִים, חוּס וְחָנֵּנוּ, וְרַחֵם עָלֵינוּ, וְהוֹשִׁיעֵנוּ כִּי אֵלֶיךָ עֵינֵינוּ, כִּי אֵל חַנּוּן וְרַחוּם אָתָּה.

וּבְנֵה יְרוּשָׁלַיִם עִיר הַקֹּדֶשׁ בִּמְהֵרָה בְיָמֵינוּ.
בָּרוּךְ אַתָּה יהוה בּוֹנֵה בְרַחֲמָיו יְרוּשָׁלָיִם. אָמֵן.

And rebuild Jerusalem, the sacred city, with speed and in our days. You are blessed, Lord, who in His mercy rebuilds Jerusalem. Amen.

1915

The poet Rainer Maria Rilke describes "The Death of Moses" (Deut. 31-33): "Then the ancient God to the ancient man slowly inclined His ancient face. In a kiss took him into His age, the older. And with hands of creation He closed the mountain. So that only the one, one re-created, should lie under terrestrial mountains, unknowable to mankind."

Mercy—Lord God-of-Us

—upon Israel, Your nation, and on Jerusalem, Your city, and on Zion, the seat of Your honor, and on the kingdom of the House of David, Your anointed one, and on the grand and holy house that is named with Your name upon it. God-of-Us, our father, nurture us, nourish us, sustain us, provide for us, and offer us leeway; and release us—Lord God-of-Us—in haste, from all our pains. And, prithee, don't put us in a situation of wanting, Lord God-of-Us, neither for handouts from flesh and blood, nor for hands bearing loans, for it is only by Your hand—the full, the open, the sacred and wide open—that we won't be ashamed and we won't be humiliated, eternally and on.

On Shabbat, add: Find favor and fortify us, Lord God-of-Us, with Your mitzvot, and with the mitzvot of the seventh day, this resplendent and sacred Shabbat. For this is a day resplendent and sacred before You, one to settle into and rest on, with love, as is the obligation born of Your will. By Your will, we were put into a state of repose, Lord God-of-Us, where there be not suffering, sorrow, nor woe on the day of our rest. And show us, Lord God-of-Us, the solace of Your city, Zion, and the rebuilding of Your holy city, Jerusalem, because You are He, Master of Reclamations, Master of Consolations.

God-of-Us and God of our fathers,

may Your memories and reminiscence of us rise up before You, reach You and be seen by You, be viewed favorably and be heard, reminisced and remembered, along with the memories of our fathers, and the memories of the Messiah, son of David, Your servant, and the memory of Jerusalem, Your holy city, and the memory of Your whole nation, the house of Israel, all set before You as a deliverance and delight, in a graceful, kindly, and merciful manner, aimed toward life and toward peace on the day of this Festival of Matzot. Remember us during it—Lord God-of-Us—positively, and reminisce about us, during it, blessedly, and bring us salvation, during it, vigorously. And through your message of salvation and compassion, show forbearance and favor, and have mercy upon us. Be the one to save us—for our eyes are toward You, for You are a true God, compassionate and merciful.

1918

On a French
postcard, Karl Marx
is depicted as "the
Modern Moses" atop
"Mount Proletariat,"
holding the "New
Tablets of the
Law": *Capital* and
*The Communist
Manifesto.*

בָּרוּךְ אַתָּה יְהֹוָה, אֱלֹהֵינוּ מֶלֶךְ הָעוֹלָם, הָאֵל, אָבִינוּ, מַלְכֵּנוּ, אַדִּירֵנוּ,
בּוֹרְאֵנוּ, גּוֹאֲלֵנוּ, יוֹצְרֵנוּ, קְדוֹשֵׁנוּ, קְדוֹשׁ יַעֲקֹב, רוֹעֵנוּ
רוֹעֵה יִשְׂרָאֵל, הַמֶּלֶךְ הַטּוֹב וְהַמֵּטִיב לַכֹּל, שֶׁבְּכָל יוֹם וָיוֹם, הוּא הֵטִיב,
הוּא מֵטִיב, הוּא יֵיטִיב לָנוּ. הוּא גְמָלָנוּ, הוּא גוֹמְלֵנוּ, הוּא יִגְמְלֵנוּ לָעַד, לְחֵן,
לְחֶסֶד, וּלְרַחֲמִים, וּלְרֶוַח הַצָּלָה וְהַצְלָחָה, בְּרָכָה וִישׁוּעָה, נֶחָמָה,
פַּרְנָסָה, וְכַלְכָּלָה, וְרַחֲמִים, וְחַיִּים, וְשָׁלוֹם וְכָל טוֹב, וּמִכָּל טוּב אַל יְחַסְּרֵנוּ.

הָרַחֲמָן,	הוּא יִמְלֹךְ עָלֵינוּ לְעוֹלָם וָעֶד.
הָרַחֲמָן,	הוּא יִתְבָּרַךְ בַּשָּׁמַיִם וּבָאָרֶץ.
הָרַחֲמָן,	הוּא יִשְׁתַּבַּח לְדוֹר דּוֹרִים, וְיִתְפָּאַר בָּנוּ לָעַד וּלְנֵצַח נְצָחִים, וְיִתְהַדַּר בָּנוּ לָעַד וּלְעוֹלְמֵי עוֹלָמִים.
הָרַחֲמָן,	הוּא יְפַרְנְסֵנוּ בְּכָבוֹד.
הָרַחֲמָן,	הוּא יִשְׁבֹּר עֻלֵּנוּ מֵעַל צַוָּארֵנוּ, וְהוּא יוֹלִיכֵנוּ קוֹמְמִיּוּת לְאַרְצֵנוּ.
הָרַחֲמָן,	הוּא יִשְׁלַח לָנוּ בְּרָכָה מְרֻבָּה בַּבַּיִת הַזֶּה, וְעַל שֻׁלְחָן זֶה שֶׁאָכַלְנוּ עָלָיו.
הָרַחֲמָן,	הוּא יִשְׁלַח לָנוּ אֶת אֵלִיָּהוּ הַנָּבִיא, זָכוּר לַטּוֹב, וִיבַשֶּׂר לָנוּ בְּשׂוֹרוֹת טוֹבוֹת, יְשׁוּעוֹת וְנֶחָמוֹת.
הָרַחֲמָן,	הוּא יְבָרֵךְ אֶת (אָבִי מוֹרִי) בַּעַל הַבַּיִת הַזֶּה, וְאֶת (אִמִּי מוֹרָתִי) בַּעֲלַת הַבַּיִת הַזֶּה, אוֹתָם וְאֶת בֵּיתָם (וְאֶת זַרְעָם) וְאֶת כָּל אֲשֶׁר לָהֶם, אוֹתָנוּ וְאֶת כָּל אֲשֶׁר לָנוּ וְאֶת כָּל הַמְסֻבִּין כָּאן, כְּמוֹ שֶׁנִּתְבָּרְכוּ אֲבוֹתֵינוּ אַבְרָהָם יִצְחָק וְיַעֲקֹב בַּכֹּל מִכֹּל כֹּל. כֵּן יְבָרֵךְ אוֹתָנוּ כֻּלָּנוּ יַחַד בִּבְרָכָה שְׁלֵמָה, וְנֹאמַר אָמֵן.

1919

Franz Kafka composes a letter to his father, writing: "I could not understand how, with the insignificant scrap of Judaism you yourself possessed, you could reproach me for not making an effort...to cling to a similar, insignificant scrap. It was...a mere nothing, a joke—not even a joke...at home it was...confined to the first Seder, which more and more developed into a farce, with fits of hysterical laughter.... How one could do anything better with that material than get rid of it as fast as possible...precisely the getting rid of it seemed to me to be the devoutest action."

You are blessed, Lord God-of-Us, King of the Cosmos, God, our Father, our King, our Majesty, our Creator, our Redeemer, our Fashioner, our Consecrator—Holy to Jacob; our Shepherd—Shepherd of Israel, the Good King Who Makes Good for All, He who—on every day, day after day—has made good, He who makes good, He who will make good for us. He who rewarded us, He who rewards us, He who will reward us eternally—with grace, with benevolence, with mercy, and with relief, through deliverance and the triumph in its wake, a blessing and a salvation, a consolation, a provision, and support, with mercy, life, peace, and all goodness. And from all goodness, do not leave us wanting.

If with one's parents, add the words in brackets.

Compassionate One, may He reign over us forever and on.

Compassionate One, may He be blessed in the heavens and on earth.

Compassionate One, may He be lauded through the ages, and be glorified through us forever and ever evermore, and made splendorous through us forever and forever everlasting.

Compassionate One, may He sustain us with dignity.

Compassionate One, may He break the yokes from our necks, and lead us to our land, our heads held high.

Compassionate One, may He send abundant blessings into this house, and onto this table from which we've partaken.

Compassionate One, may He send us Elijah the Prophet, who is remembered well, and who will bear glad tidings, salvations, and consolations.

Compassionate One, may He bless [my father, my teacher,] the master of this house, and [my mother, my teacher,] the mistress of this house, them and their home [and their offspring] and all that belongs to them—us, and all that belongs to us, and all who are reclining here—in the way in which our fathers, Abraham, Isaac, and Jacob, were blessed: with all, of all, all. Thus, may He bless us together as one, with an overarching blessing, and let us all say, Amen.

In James Joyce's *Ulysses*, Leopold Bloom is struck by a memory of Passover on his walk through Dublin: "AND IT WAS THE FEAST OF THE PASSOVER.... Poor papa with his hagadah book, reading backwards with his finger to me. Pessach. Next year in Jerusalem. Dear, O dear! All that long business about that brought us out of the land of Egypt and into the house of bondage *Alleluia. Shema Israel Adonai Elohenu...*And then the lamb and the cat and the dog and the stick and the water and the butcher.... Sounds a bit silly till you come to look into it well."

בַּמָּרוֹם יְלַמְּדוּ עֲלֵיהֶם וְעָלֵינוּ זְכוּת שֶׁתְּהִי לְמִשְׁמֶרֶת שָׁלוֹם. וְנִשָּׂא בְרָכָה מֵאֵת יהוה וּצְדָקָה מֵאֱלֹהֵי יִשְׁעֵנוּ, וְנִמְצָא חֵן וְשֵׂכֶל טוֹב בְּעֵינֵי אֱלֹהִים וְאָדָם.

[הָרַחֲמָן, הוּא יַנְחִילֵנוּ יוֹם שֶׁכֻּלּוֹ שַׁבָּת וּמְנוּחָה לְחַיֵּי הָעוֹלָמִים.]

הָרַחֲמָן, הוּא יַנְחִילֵנוּ יוֹם שֶׁכֻּלּוֹ טוֹב, יוֹם שֶׁכֻּלּוֹ אָרוּךְ, יוֹם שֶׁצַּדִּיקִים יוֹשְׁבִים וְעַטְרוֹתֵיהֶם בְּרָאשֵׁיהֶם וְנֶהֱנִים מִזִּיו הַשְּׁכִינָה, וְיִהְיֶה חֶלְקֵנוּ עִמָּהֶם.

הָרַחֲמָן, הוּא יְזַכֵּנוּ לִימוֹת הַמָּשִׁיחַ וּלְחַיֵּי הָעוֹלָם הַבָּא. מִגְדּוֹל יְשׁוּעוֹת מַלְכּוֹ וְעֹשֶׂה חֶסֶד לִמְשִׁיחוֹ לְדָוִד וּלְזַרְעוֹ עַד עוֹלָם. עֹשֶׂה שָׁלוֹם בִּמְרוֹמָיו הוּא יַעֲשֶׂה שָׁלוֹם עָלֵינוּ וְעַל כָּל יִשְׂרָאֵל, וְאִמְרוּ אָמֵן.

יְראוּ אֶת יהוה

קְדֹשָׁיו, כִּי אֵין מַחְסוֹר לִירֵאָיו. כְּפִירִים רָשׁוּ וְרָעֵבוּ, דֹּרְשֵׁי יהוה לֹא יַחְסְרוּ כָל טוֹב.

הוֹדוּ לַיהוה כִּי טוֹב, כִּי לְעוֹלָם חַסְדּוֹ. פּוֹתֵחַ אֶת יָדֶךָ וּמַשְׂבִּיעַ לְכָל חַי רָצוֹן. בָּרוּךְ הַגֶּבֶר אֲשֶׁר יִבְטַח בַּיהוה, וְהָיָה יהוה מִבְטַחוֹ. נַעַר הָיִיתִי גַּם זָקַנְתִּי, וְלֹא רָאִיתִי צַדִּיק נֶעֱזָב, וְזַרְעוֹ מְבַקֶּשׁ לָחֶם. יהוה עֹז לְעַמּוֹ יִתֵּן, יהוה יְבָרֵךְ אֶת עַמּוֹ בַשָּׁלוֹם.

מַה שֶּׁאָכַלְנוּ יִהְיֶה לְשָׂבְעָה
וּמַה שֶּׁשָּׁתִינוּ יִהְיֶה לִרְפוּאָה.
וּמַה שֶּׁהוֹתַרְנוּ יִהְיֶה לִבְרָכָה, כְּדִכְתִיב
וַיִּתֵּן לִפְנֵיהֶם וַיֹּאכְלוּ וַיּוֹתִירוּ כִּדְבַר יהוה.

Ras Tafari Makonnen is crowned emperor of Ethiopia under the name Haile Selassie. Many black Jamaicans interpret Selassie's ascendance as the fulfillment of Marcus Garvey's command to "look to Africa where a Black king shall be crowned, he shall be your redeemer." They develop a new religion, Rastafarianism, which views Selassie as a messiah who will lead the black race to liberation. Rastafarians identify with the plight of the Hebrew slaves in Egypt, calling Africa "Zion" and the black Diaspora "Babylon." To obey the Old Testament, they adhere to Jewish dietary laws and refrain from cutting their hair.

Through the heavens, may He cast His favor upon them and upon us, cocooning us in peace. And may we bear a blessing from the Lord and a beneficence from the God of our salvation, and may we find grace and wisdom in the eyes of God and man.

On Shabbat, add this sentence: **[Compassionate One,** may He confer on us a day, the whole of it Shabbat and rest, for life eternal.]

Compassionate One, may He confer on us a day, the whole of it good, a day that is one long extended perfection, a day when the righteous sit, coronets on their heads, enjoying the luminary splendor of the Divine Presence, may our portions be with them.

Compassionate One, may He grant us the era of the Messiah and the eternal life of the world to come. He who is the tower of salvation for His king, and shows benevolence to His anointed, David, and his offspring forever forward. He who makes peace in the heavens, may He rain peace down upon us, and on all of Israel, and now we say, Amen.

May His holy ones

revere the Lord, for those in awe of Him will face no shortage. Lion cubs go wanting, they go famished, while seekers of the Lord will not lack. Thank the Lord because He is good, because His benevolence is never-ending. Open Your hand and sate the needs of all living things. Blessed is the robust man who entrusts himself to the Lord, and the Lord will be his protector. I was once a boy, now I've aged, and I never saw one of the righteous forsaken or his offspring ask for bread. May the Lord give might to His nation, may the Lord bless His nation with peace.

What we ate should leave us sated. And what we drank should be for a remedy. And what remains should be for a blessing, as it is written: *And he set down before them, and they ate, and they left over, according to the word of the Lord.*

כּוֹס שְׁלִישִׁי

הִנְנִי מוּכָן/מוּכָנָה וּמְזֻמָּן/וּמְזֻמֶּנֶת לְקַיֵּם
מִצְוַת כּוֹס שְׁלִישִׁי שֶׁהוּא כְּנֶגֶד בְּשׂוֹרַת
הַיְשׁוּעָה שֶׁאָמַר הַקָּדוֹשׁ בָּרוּךְ הוּא
לְיִשְׂרָאֵל: וְגָאַלְתִּי אֶתְכֶם בִּזְרוֹעַ נְטוּיָה
וּבִשְׁפָטִים גְּדוֹלִים.

בָּרוּךְ אַתָּה יהוה, אֱלֹהֵינוּ מֶלֶךְ הָעוֹלָם,
בּוֹרֵא פְּרִי הַגָּפֶן.

Third Cup

Raise the cup of wine and recite:

Here I am, prepared and ardent, allied and present, ready to perform the mitzvah of the third cup, the enactment of salvation's promise. As the Holy One, Blessed is He, declared to Israel: *And I will redeem you with an outstretched arm and formidable judgments.*

You are blessed, Lord God-of-Us, King of the Cosmos, Maker of the fruit of the vine.

While reclining, drink at least most of the cup.

In Syria, archaeologists discover the Dura Europos synagogue. Built in the 3rd century, the synagogue has extraordinary wall frescoes that draw upon both Jewish and Greek mythology, and include a depiction of Moses being drawn out of the water by Aphrodite. Tonight, the fresco is in the National Museum of Damascus.

שְׁפֹךְ חֲמָתְךָ אֶל הַגּוֹיִם אֲשֶׁר לֹא יְדָעוּךָ, וְעַל מַמְלָכוֹת אֲשֶׁר בְּשִׁמְךָ לֹא קָרָאוּ. כִּי אָכַל אֶת יַעֲקֹב, וְאֶת נָוֵהוּ הֵשַׁמּוּ. שְׁפָךְ עֲלֵיהֶם זַעְמֶךָ, וַחֲרוֹן אַפְּךָ יַשִּׂיגֵם. תִּרְדֹּף בְּאַף וְתַשְׁמִידֵם, מִתַּחַת שְׁמֵי יהוה.

Fill the fourth cup, as well as the Cup of Elijah. Send someone to open the door. Once it is opened, recite together:

Shed your wrath upon the nations that do not recognize You, and on the kingdoms that will not proclaim Your name. For they devoured Jacob, and his dominion they laid bare. Pour upon them Your indignation and let Your rage engulf them. Pursue them in anger and annihilate them from under the heavens of the Lord.

Polish Zionists commemorate Passover with a satirical Haggadah titled "Kulo Maror" ("Only Bitter Herbs"). It features a dish concocted of "Hitlerism," "Racial theory," and "Discriminatory economic measures against Polish Jews."

A cartoon below the seder plate shows Zionist leader Ze'ev Jabotinsky pleading with a modern Pharaoh—depicted as the King of England—to allow Jews to immigrate to British Palestine.

The German poet Karl Wolfskehl writes: "Again, again, when we, covered with the journey's dust/ Rested, tired, in a stranger's bower/ The others roughly lifted us and threatened/ Again and again."

ehold, I will send you Elijah the Prophet in advance of the momentous, awe-inspiring Day of the Lord. He will turn the hearts of fathers back toward their sons, the hearts of sons back toward their fathers.

Elijah the Prophet, Elijah the Tishbi,
Elijah, Elijah, Elijah the Giladi,
let him come to us with speed and in our days,
with the Messiah, son of David.

הִנֵּה אָנֹכִי שֹׁלֵחַ לָכֶם אֵת אֵלִיָּה הַנָּבִיא, לִפְנֵי בּוֹא יוֹם יהוה הַגָּדוֹל וְהַנּוֹרָא. וְהֵשִׁיב לֵב אָבוֹת עַל בָּנִים, וְלֵב בָּנִים עַל אֲבוֹתָם.

אֵלִיָּהוּ הַנָּבִיא, אֵלִיָּהוּ הַתִּשְׁבִּי, אֵלִיָּהוּ, אֵלִיָּהוּ, אֵלִיָּהוּ הַגִּלְעָדִי, בִּמְהֵרָה בְיָמֵינוּ יָבֹא אֵלֵינוּ עִם מָשִׁיחַ בֶּן דָּוִד.

Close the door.

"You shall not wrong a stranger or oppress him, for you were strangers in the land of Egypt." Exodus 22:20

He is the beggar on the side of the road, the servant, and the harlot. He is also the Roman official, the Persian, and the Arab. He is, above all, the stranger.

Elijah the Prophet appears in all of these guises as he wanders the world according to Jewish tradition. In most of the tales devoted to him—and revealingly, more Jewish folktales are told about Elijah than any other figure—he shows up where we least expect him, often becoming the object of our insults before his true identity is revealed.

House of Study

Thus, the Babylonian Talmud tells the story of Rabbi Shimon son of Eleazar, who was once returning from his teacher, full of pride at the amount of Torah that he had learned. On the way, Rabbi Shimon encountered Elijah, disguised as an exceptionally ugly man. "Peace be upon you, Rabbi," Elijah greeted the sage. "Empty one," the sage responded, "how ugly you are. Is everyone in your town so ugly?" "I do not know," said the man. "Why don't you go and tell the craftsman who made me how ugly is the vessel that he has created?" Realizing his sin, Rabbi Shimon dismounted the donkey he was riding and followed Elijah, begging his forgiveness.

For Rabbi Shimon, his encounter with Elijah revealed a different stranger—the ultimate stranger—God. Tonight, who is the stranger that Elijah reveals to us?

We interrupt this celebration of liberation to bring you a word from the Jewish id. "Pour out Thy Wrath,"

we demand of God. But wait. We moderns have been told that we are opening the door for Elijah as a way of signaling our readiness to work for a better time, a messianic age free of strife and unfairness. Aren't we opening the door to the poor, and to the people of all nations, inviting them to come eat with us and learn with us? Well, yes, but we open doors, and close doors, for many reasons. In the ghettos of Europe, Jews opened their doors at this moment in the seder for two fascinating and conflicting reasons. One was to let the gentiles see that, yes, indeed, the Jews were doing what they claimed they were doing, having an innocent meal together—no Christian children being slaughtered here, thank you very much. At the same time, employing words not understood by their neighbors, the Jews were venting their anger at the gentiles who were making their lives a misery.

The anger of our ghetto ancestors was understandable. Why not let powerless people have their fantasies of justice and revenge? But should we pour out our wrath today, onto societies that accept us? Or, to ask the question another way, is righteous anger, even aimed at ancient enemies, and not our neighbors, ennobling or distorting? Anger, channeled destructively, can lead to vindictiveness, to a kind of constricting tribalism that sees everyone on the other side of our circled wagons as an enemy. Destructive anger is one of the great dangers of our age. Technology has, among other things, enabled the instantaneous transmission of invective; the Internet is used all too often to demonize and polarize. The Talmud tells us that God loves the man who does not get angry.

Nation

But isn't anger also a useful motivator? Isn't there such a thing as righteous anger? The abolitionists were angry; the suffragists were angry; Herzl was angry; Gandhi was angry. But they poured their wrath not into vengeful violence, but into new foundations of justice. But how do we know when our constructive anger becomes dangerous? Can we ever trust our emotions? Or is that why we have law—because we can't?

Elijah the Prophet

It is difficult not to be jealous of Elijah, who for many years held the enviable job of prophet and who now is welcomed in any civilized home, ushered in through the door and served immediate refreshment. (Consider, in comparison, the

Playground

sad case of Santa Claus, a figure from a more prominent and less interesting religion, who is forced to enter homes via the chimney and must bribe the residents with gifts if he expects any kindness before returning to his home in one of the least habitable regions of the globe.)

Like many prophets, Elijah is invisible and silent, so if you are one of the people asked to go open the door for him, rather than the people who stay behind at the table to "check on the wine," you can think up the sort of conversation you might have with Elijah and reply out loud with statements such as "What a handsome vest, Elijah!" or "Elijah, it really seems like you've had more than enough wine for one evening," or even "Certainly, Elijah, I'd love to take a ride in your automobile, just let me get my coat," and soon everyone in the house will be rushing to the door in the hopes of catching a glimpse of him.

Diverse religious impulses animate the figure of Elijah. The prophet lived during the reign of King Ahab and his foreign queen, Jezebel, and he was fierce in defense of the people's faith, hurling denunciations at the people's seduction by the queen's alien god and arranging a showdown with the rival priests, whom he then slaughtered. "Seize the prophets of Baal," he cried out in his victory. "Let none of them escape!"

But the Jewish imagination transformed the zealot into the most familiar of biblical characters, the hero of countless tales of fantasy told in every country in which Jews have lived. All through the lands of the Sephardim and the Levant, traversing the Pale of Settlement of Eastern Europe and Russia, leaping across the oceans to the New World: wherever Jews have wandered, so wanders the storyteller's Elijah. He appears

Library

mysteriously and performs his miracles on behalf of the most humbled and the most threatened. He's more an imp than an avenger, inserting himself as the only barrier between the defenseless and their doom. Usually he's disguised as a beggar or a vagabond. In "The Conjuror," a story by the Yiddish master Y.L. Peretz, he arrives in town and rents a huge hall to amaze the people with his flashy magic tricks and also with his marginal existence: "A man scrapes ducats off the sole of his boot, and he can't even afford a room at the inn. He merely whistles to bake up loaves of challah...and yet his face looks like he just stepped out of a coffin, and his eyes are ablaze with hunger." There are powerful paradoxes impressed into this figure, prodding us into asking what we want out of this life, which of our hungers should be unappeasable.

The Haggadah's fiery words, recited as the door stands open for the prophet, conjure up the prophet of Scripture, formidable in his certitude and seeking his justice in vengeance. Other emotions went into the storyteller's Elijah who roams the earth, as intimate to those who await him as Jewish grieving and Jewish dreaming. When we open the door, which of the Elijahs are we hoping will enter?

The Joseph Jacobs
advertising
agency launches a
marketing campaign
for Maxwell House
Coffee, obtaining
certification that
the brand is kosher
for Passover and
distributing a free
Haggadah with
purchase. The
Maxwell House
Haggadah becomes
an annual fixture
in American
Jewish culture,
and more than 40
million copies are
distributed in the
United States.

הַלֵּל

לֹא לָנוּ יהוה לֹא לָנוּ

כִּי לְשִׁמְךָ תֵּן כָּבוֹד

עַל חַסְדְּךָ עַל אֲמִתֶּךָ.

לָמָּה יֹאמְרוּ הַגּוֹיִם

אַיֵּה נָא אֱלֹהֵיהֶם.

וֵאלֹהֵינוּ בַשָּׁמַיִם

כֹּל אֲשֶׁר חָפֵץ עָשָׂה.

עֲצַבֵּיהֶם כֶּסֶף וְזָהָב

מַעֲשֵׂה יְדֵי אָדָם.

פֶּה לָהֶם וְלֹא יְדַבֵּרוּ

עֵינַיִם לָהֶם וְלֹא יִרְאוּ.

אָזְנַיִם לָהֶם וְלֹא יִשְׁמָעוּ

אַף לָהֶם וְלֹא יְרִיחוּן.

יְדֵיהֶם וְלֹא יְמִישׁוּן

רַגְלֵיהֶם וְלֹא יְהַלֵּכוּ

לֹא יֶהְגּוּ בִּגְרוֹנָם.

כְּמוֹהֶם יִהְיוּ עֹשֵׂיהֶם

כֹּל אֲשֶׁר בֹּטֵחַ בָּהֶם.

יִשְׂרָאֵל בְּטַח בַּיהוה

עֶזְרָם וּמָגִנָּם הוּא.

בֵּית אַהֲרֹן בִּטְחוּ בַיהוה

עֶזְרָם וּמָגִנָּם הוּא.

יִרְאֵי יהוה בִּטְחוּ בַיהוה

עֶזְרָם וּמָגִנָּם הוּא.

יהוה זְכָרָנוּ יְבָרֵךְ

יְבָרֵךְ אֶת בֵּית יִשְׂרָאֵל

יְבָרֵךְ אֶת בֵּית אַהֲרֹן

יְבָרֵךְ יִרְאֵי יהוה

הַקְּטַנִּים עִם הַגְּדֹלִים

יֹסֵף יהוה עֲלֵיכֶם

עֲלֵיכֶם וְעַל בְּנֵיכֶם.

בְּרוּכִים אַתֶּם לַיהוה

עֹשֵׂה שָׁמַיִם וָאָרֶץ.

הַשָּׁמַיִם שָׁמַיִם לַיהוה

וְהָאָרֶץ נָתַן לִבְנֵי אָדָם.

לֹא הַמֵּתִים יְהַלְלוּ יָהּ

וְלֹא כָּל יֹרְדֵי דוּמָה.

וַאֲנַחְנוּ נְבָרֵךְ יָהּ

מֵעַתָּה וְעַד עוֹלָם. הַלְלוּיָהּ.

In *Mules and Men*, her collection of stories based on African-American folk traditions, the writer Zora Neale Hurston tells a tale: "Moses talked with the snake that lives in a hole right under God's footrest. Moses had fire in his head and a cloud in his mouth. The snake had told him God's making words....Many a man thinks he is making something when he's only changing things around. But God let Moses make. And then Moses had so much power he made the eight winged angels split open a mountain to bury him in, and shut up the hole behind them."

Hallel

Not on us, Lord, not on us,
    but on Your name bestow the honor—
upon Your kindness, Your truth.
How can the nations say,
    Where, pray tell, is their God?
When our God is in heaven,
    And all that He pleases, He does.
Their idols, formed of silver and gold,
    they are the work of human hands.
A mouth to them, and they cannot speak,
    eyes to them, and they cannot see.
Ears to them, and they cannot hear,
    nose to them, and they cannot smell.
They cannot feel with their hands,
    they cannot walk on their legs,
        no sounds usher from their throat.
Like them may their makers be,
    so, too, all who trust in them.
Israel puts trust in the Lord,
    champion and shield is He.
The House of Aaron puts trust in the Lord,
    champion and shield is He.
Those who revere the Lord put trust in the Lord,
    champion and shield is He.

Lord, who keeps us in memory, bless us,
    bless the House of Israel, bless the
    House of Aaron.
Bless those who revere the Lord,
    the little ones along with the grown.
The Lord will increase you,
    you and your sons.
Blessed are you to the Lord,
    the Maker of heaven and earth.
The heavens are the heavens of the Lord,
    and the earth He granted to mankind.
No, the dead cannot praise You, God,
    nor those who sink into the silence of
    the grave.
But we will bless You, God,
    from now until the end of time.
    Hallelujah.

New York remains the world's largest Jewish city. Its Jewish population of 2,085,000, or 28% of the total, is greater than the next five largest Jewish cities—Moscow, Warsaw, Chicago, Philadelphia, and London—combined. While the majority of Jews—56.8%—still live in Europe, the United States has the largest Jewish population of any country in the world, with 4,870,000 Jewish residents.

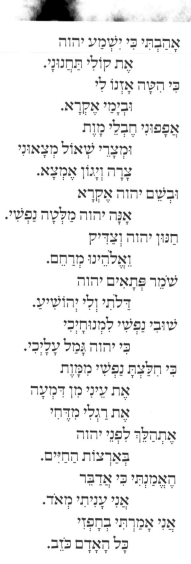

אָהַבְתִּי כִּי יִשְׁמַע יהוה
אֶת קוֹלִי תַּחֲנוּנָי.
כִּי הִטָּה אָזְנוֹ לִי
וּבְיָמַי אֶקְרָא.
אֲפָפוּנִי חֶבְלֵי מָוֶת
וּמְצָרֵי שְׁאוֹל מְצָאוּנִי
צָרָה וְיָגוֹן אֶמְצָא.
וּבְשֵׁם יהוה אֶקְרָא
אָנָּה יהוה מַלְּטָה נַפְשִׁי.
חַנּוּן יהוה וְצַדִּיק
וֵאלֹהֵינוּ מְרַחֵם.
שֹׁמֵר פְּתָאִים יהוה
דַּלּוֹתִי וְלִי יְהוֹשִׁיעַ.
שׁוּבִי נַפְשִׁי לִמְנוּחָיְכִי
כִּי יהוה גָּמַל עָלָיְכִי.
כִּי חִלַּצְתָּ נַפְשִׁי מִמָּוֶת
אֶת עֵינִי מִן דִּמְעָה
אֶת רַגְלִי מִדֶּחִי
אֶתְהַלֵּךְ לִפְנֵי יהוה
בְּאַרְצוֹת הַחַיִּים.
הֶאֱמַנְתִּי כִּי אֲדַבֵּר
אֲנִי עָנִיתִי מְאֹד.
אֲנִי אָמַרְתִּי בְחָפְזִי
כָּל הָאָדָם כֹּזֵב.

מָה אָשִׁיב לַיהוה
כָּל תַּגְמוּלוֹהִי עָלָי.
כּוֹס יְשׁוּעוֹת אֶשָּׂא
וּבְשֵׁם יהוה אֶקְרָא.
נְדָרַי לַיהוה אֲשַׁלֵּם
נֶגְדָה נָּא לְכָל עַמּוֹ.
יָקָר בְּעֵינֵי יהוה
הַמָּוְתָה לַחֲסִידָיו.
אָנָּה יהוה כִּי אֲנִי עַבְדֶּךָ
אֲנִי עַבְדְּךָ בֶּן אֲמָתֶךָ
פִּתַּחְתָּ לְמוֹסֵרָי.
לְךָ אֶזְבַּח זֶבַח תּוֹדָה
וּבְשֵׁם יהוה אֶקְרָא
נְדָרַי לַיהוה אֲשַׁלֵּם
נֶגְדָה נָּא לְכָל עַמּוֹ.
בְּחַצְרוֹת בֵּית יהוה
בְּתוֹכֵכִי יְרוּשָׁלָיִם.
הַלְלוּיָהּ.

Emanuel Ringelblum, historian of the Warsaw Ghetto, spends Passover at the home of fellow ghetto resident Shachna Zagan and gets into a debate about vengeance over dinner. Fellow guest Issac Giterman argues that "vengeance would never solve anything. The vanquished would in turn plan their own vengeance, and so it would go on forever...raising the moral level of all humanity was the only solution." Three years later, Ringelblum and his family are killed by Nazi troops.

I love the Lord because He hears

my voice, my prayers.

Because He bends His ear toward me,

and through my days I will call upon Him.

When I find myself bound by death's ties,

and the agonies of the abyss have found me,

when I am wound up in misery and grief...

In the name of the Lord, I will call,

Please, Lord, let my soul slip free.

Gracious is the Lord, and just,

our God exudes mercy.

The Lord is the guardian of the innocent,

I was brought low, and He was my savior.

My soul, return to your resting place,

because the Lord has rewarded you.

For You stripped my soul away from death,

spared my eye from the teardrop,

my leg from stumbling.

I will walk before the Lord,

in the lands of the living.

I still believed, though exclaiming,

"I suffer greatly!"

And while speaking in haste,

"All mankind are liars!"

With what will I requite the Lord,

all His benefits heaped upon me?

I will raise the cup of salvation,

and cry out in the name of the Lord.

I will fulfill my pledges to the Lord,

before the whole of His nation.

Heavy in the eyes of the Lord,

is the passing of His pious ones.

I beseech thee, Lord, for I am Your servant,

I am Your servant, son of Your handmaiden,

You opened and unbound me.

I will make an offering of thanks to You,

and cry out in the name of the Lord;

I will fulfill my pledges to the Lord,

before the whole of His nation—

In the courtyards of the house of the Lord,

in your midst, Jerusalem.

Hallelujah.

In Alsace, France, S.R. Kapel, the former rabbi of Mühlhausen, creates a Haggadah for use in the internment camps during Passover. As with all of the Haggadahs known to have been produced under the German occupation, it is written by hand on several sheets of paper and then mimeographed. In addition to the traditional last line—"Next year in Jerusalem"—the rabbi adds another: *"Die Hagodeh zol zayn die letzte in Goles!"* ("This Haggadah should be the final one in exile!")

הַלְלוּ אֶת יהוה כָּל גּוֹיִם
שַׁבְּחוּהוּ כָּל הָאֻמִּים.
כִּי גָבַר עָלֵינוּ חַסְדּוֹ
וֶאֱמֶת יהוה לְעוֹלָם.
הַלְלוּיָהּ.

הוֹדוּ לַיהוה כִּי טוֹב
כִּי לְעוֹלָם חַסְדּוֹ.
יֹאמַר נָא יִשְׂרָאֵל
כִּי לְעוֹלָם חַסְדּוֹ.
יֹאמְרוּ נָא בֵית אַהֲרֹן
כִּי לְעוֹלָם חַסְדּוֹ.
יֹאמְרוּ נָא יִרְאֵי יהוה
כִּי לְעוֹלָם חַסְדּוֹ.

מִן הַמֵּצַר קָרָאתִי יָּהּ
עָנָנִי בַמֶּרְחָב יָהּ.
יהוה לִי לֹא אִירָא
מַה יַּעֲשֶׂה לִי אָדָם.
יהוה לִי בְּעֹזְרָי
וַאֲנִי אֶרְאֶה בְשֹׂנְאָי.
טוֹב לַחֲסוֹת בַּיהוה
מִבְּטֹחַ בָּאָדָם.
טוֹב לַחֲסוֹת בַּיהוה
מִבְּטֹחַ בִּנְדִיבִים.
כָּל גּוֹיִם סְבָבוּנִי
בְּשֵׁם יהוה כִּי אֲמִילַם.
סַבּוּנִי גַם סְבָבוּנִי
בְּשֵׁם יהוה כִּי אֲמִילַם.
סַבּוּנִי כִדְבֹרִים
דֹעֲכוּ כְּאֵשׁ קוֹצִים
בְּשֵׁם יהוה כִּי אֲמִילַם.
דָּחֹה דְחִיתַנִי לִנְפֹּל
וַיהוה עֲזָרָנִי.
עָזִּי וְזִמְרָת יָהּ
וַיְהִי לִי לִישׁוּעָה.
קוֹל רִנָּה וִישׁוּעָה
בְּאָהֳלֵי צַדִּיקִים
יְמִין יהוה עֹשָׂה חָיִל.
יְמִין יהוה רוֹמֵמָה
יְמִין יהוה עֹשָׂה חָיִל.
לֹא אָמוּת כִּי אֶחְיֶה
וַאֲסַפֵּר מַעֲשֵׂי יָהּ.

William Faulkner's *Go Down, Moses*, named after the African-American spiritual based on Exodus 7:16, explores the complicated legacy of race and slavery in the pre– and post–Civil War South.

All nations praise the Lord,
    Let Him be lauded by all people,
Because His kindness overpowered us,
    and the truth of the Lord is eternal.
Hallelujah.

Thanks to the Lord for He is good,
    everlasting is His lovingkindness.
Say thus, Israel,
    everlasting is His lovingkindness.
Say thus, House of Aaron,
    everlasting is His lovingkindness.
Say thus, those who revere the Lord,
    everlasting is His lovingkindness.

From the tightening straits I called to God,
    He answered me with Godly expanse.
The Lord is with me, I will not fear,
    what harm can man bring to me?
The Lord supports me through my allies,
    and so I face my enemies.
Better to rely on the Lord,
    than to trust in man.
Better to rely on the Lord,
    than to trust in noblemen.
I am surrounded by all nations,
    in the name of the Lord, I will crush
    them like dried leaves.
They surround me and keep on surrounding,
    in the name of the Lord, I will crush
    them like dried leaves.
They swarm around me like bees,
    and are extinguished like a thicket of
    thorns on fire,
    in the name of the Lord, I will crush them
    like dried leaves.
Pushed—they pushed me near to falling,
    and the Lord came to my rescue.
God is my strength and my song,
    and He was, for me, salvation.
This is the sound of happy song and salvation,
    in the tents of the righteous:
        The right hand of the Lord is might making.
The right hand of the Lord is raised high,
    The right hand of the Lord is might making.
I will not die so I may live,
    and recount the deeds of God.

In June, the German-
born theologian
Martin Buber,
writing in exile from
Palestine, completes
his study of Moses:
"What is important
for us about this
God of Moses is...He
makes His demand
that the people
shall be...a people
whose entire life is
hallowed by justice
and loyalty, a people
for God and for
the world.... That
Moses experienced
Him in this fashion
and serves Him
accordingly is what
has set that man
apart as a living and
effective force at
all times, and that
is what places him
thus afresh in our
day, which possibly
requires him more
than any earlier day
has ever done."

יַסֹּר יִסְּרַנִּי יָהּ
וְלַמָּוֶת לֹא נְתָנָנִי.
פִּתְחוּ לִי שַׁעֲרֵי צֶדֶק
אָבֹא בָם אוֹדֶה יָהּ.
זֶה הַשַּׁעַר לַיהוה
צַדִּיקִים יָבֹאוּ בוֹ.

אוֹדְךָ כִּי עֲנִיתָנִי
וַתְּהִי לִי לִישׁוּעָה
אֶבֶן מָאֲסוּ הַבּוֹנִים
הָיְתָה לְרֹאשׁ פִּנָּה.
מֵאֵת יהוה הָיְתָה זֹּאת
הִיא נִפְלָאת בְּעֵינֵינוּ.
זֶה הַיּוֹם עָשָׂה יהוה
נָגִילָה וְנִשְׂמְחָה בוֹ.

אָנָּא יהוה הוֹשִׁיעָה נָּא.
אָנָּא יהוה הוֹשִׁיעָה נָּא.
אָנָּא יהוה הַצְלִיחָה נָּא.
אָנָּא יהוה הַצְלִיחָה נָּא.

בָּרוּךְ הַבָּא בְּשֵׁם יהוה
בֵּרַכְנוּכֶם מִבֵּית יהוה.
אֵל יהוה וַיָּאֶר לָנוּ
אִסְרוּ חַג בַּעֲבֹתִים
עַד קַרְנוֹת הַמִּזְבֵּחַ.
אֵלִי אַתָּה וְאוֹדֶךָּ
אֱלֹהַי אֲרוֹמְמֶךָּ.
הוֹדוּ לַיהוה כִּי טוֹב
כִּי לְעוֹלָם חַסְדּוֹ.

1946

Outside Munich, in a displaced persons camp in American-occupied Germany, survivors of the Holocaust create a Haggadah intertwining the stories of the Exodus and the fate of European Jewry for their first postwar Passover. It is forgotten until 2000, when Saul Touster finds a copy among his father's papers and arranges for its publication.

1945

While fighting on German soil, the 42nd Infantry "Rainbow" Division prints a Haggadah for its seder. The soldiers who print it use Nazi flags to clean the press.

Chastened—God chastened me,
and He did not give me over to death.
Open the Gates of Righteousness for me,
I will walk through them, thanking God.
This is the gate to the Lord,
the righteous shall walk through.

Repeat twice: I will give thanks to You for having
answered me, You are my salvation.

Repeat twice: The stone the builders rejected,
it came to be the cornerstone.

Repeat twice: This was the Lord's doing,
it is wondrous in our eyes.

Repeat twice: This day was made by the Lord,
we will revel and rejoice in it.

Lord, please save us.
Lord, please save us.
Lord, let us prosper.
Lord, let us prosper.

Repeat twice: Blessed is the one who comes in the name of
the Lord;
we bless You from the House of the Lord.

Repeat twice: God is the Lord and He shines upon us;
leash the festival sacrifice with ropes
to the horns of the altar.

Repeat twice: You are my God and I will give thanks to You;
my God, I will extol you.

Repeat twice: Thanks to the Lord for He is good,
everlasting is His lovingkindness.

יְהַלְלוּךָ יהוה אֱלֹהֵינוּ כָּל מַעֲשֶׂיךָ, וַחֲסִידֶיךָ צַדִּיקִים עוֹשֵׂי רְצוֹנֶךָ וְכָל עַמְּךָ בֵּית יִשְׂרָאֵל, בְּרִנָּה יוֹדוּ וִיבָרְכוּ וִישַׁבְּחוּ וִיפָאֲרוּ וִירוֹמְמוּ וְיַעֲרִיצוּ וְיַקְדִּישׁוּ וְיַמְלִיכוּ אֶת שִׁמְךָ מַלְכֵּנוּ. כִּי לְךָ טוֹב לְהוֹדוֹת וּלְשִׁמְךָ נָאֶה לְזַמֵּר, כִּי מֵעוֹלָם וְעַד עוֹלָם אַתָּה אֵל.

כִּי לְעוֹלָם חַסְדּוֹ.	הוֹדוּ לַיהוה כִּי טוֹב
כִּי לְעוֹלָם חַסְדּוֹ.	הוֹדוּ לֵאלֹהֵי הָאֱלֹהִים
כִּי לְעוֹלָם חַסְדּוֹ.	הוֹדוּ לַאֲדֹנֵי הָאֲדֹנִים
כִּי לְעוֹלָם חַסְדּוֹ.	לְעֹשֵׂה נִפְלָאוֹת גְּדֹלוֹת לְבַדּוֹ
כִּי לְעוֹלָם חַסְדּוֹ.	לְעֹשֵׂה הַשָּׁמַיִם בִּתְבוּנָה
כִּי לְעוֹלָם חַסְדּוֹ.	לְרֹקַע הָאָרֶץ עַל הַמָּיִם
כִּי לְעוֹלָם חַסְדּוֹ.	לְעֹשֵׂה אוֹרִים גְּדֹלִים
כִּי לְעוֹלָם חַסְדּוֹ.	אֶת הַשֶּׁמֶשׁ לְמֶמְשֶׁלֶת בַּיּוֹם
כִּי לְעוֹלָם חַסְדּוֹ.	אֶת הַיָּרֵחַ וְכוֹכָבִים לְמֶמְשְׁלוֹת בַּלָּיְלָה
כִּי לְעוֹלָם חַסְדּוֹ.	לְמַכֵּה מִצְרַיִם בִּבְכוֹרֵיהֶם
כִּי לְעוֹלָם חַסְדּוֹ.	וַיּוֹצֵא יִשְׂרָאֵל מִתּוֹכָם
כִּי לְעוֹלָם חַסְדּוֹ.	בְּיָד חֲזָקָה וּבִזְרוֹעַ נְטוּיָה
כִּי לְעוֹלָם חַסְדּוֹ.	לְגֹזֵר יַם סוּף לִגְזָרִים
כִּי לְעוֹלָם חַסְדּוֹ.	וְהֶעֱבִיר יִשְׂרָאֵל בְּתוֹכוֹ
כִּי לְעוֹלָם חַסְדּוֹ.	וְנִעֵר פַּרְעֹה וְחֵילוֹ בְיַם סוּף
כִּי לְעוֹלָם חַסְדּוֹ.	לְמוֹלִיךְ עַמּוֹ בַּמִּדְבָּר
כִּי לְעוֹלָם חַסְדּוֹ.	לְמַכֵּה מְלָכִים גְּדֹלִים
כִּי לְעוֹלָם חַסְדּוֹ.	וַיַּהֲרֹג מְלָכִים אַדִּירִים
כִּי לְעוֹלָם חַסְדּוֹ.	לְסִיחוֹן מֶלֶךְ הָאֱמֹרִי
כִּי לְעוֹלָם חַסְדּוֹ.	וּלְעוֹג מֶלֶךְ הַבָּשָׁן
כִּי לְעוֹלָם חַסְדּוֹ.	וְנָתַן אַרְצָם לְנַחֲלָה
כִּי לְעוֹלָם חַסְדּוֹ.	נַחֲלָה לְיִשְׂרָאֵל עַבְדּוֹ
כִּי לְעוֹלָם חַסְדּוֹ.	שֶׁבְּשִׁפְלֵנוּ זָכַר לָנוּ
כִּי לְעוֹלָם חַסְדּוֹ.	וַיִּפְרְקֵנוּ מִצָּרֵינוּ
כִּי לְעוֹלָם חַסְדּוֹ.	נֹתֵן לֶחֶם לְכָל בָּשָׂר
כִּי לְעוֹלָם חַסְדּוֹ.	הוֹדוּ לְאֵל הַשָּׁמָיִם

On July 11, a ship named *Exodus 1947* leaves the French port of Sète with 4,500 survivors of the Holocaust. Bound for Palestine, the ship is intercepted by the British Royal Navy, and the survivors are deported to Germany. The incident provokes international outrage and intensifies the pressure on the United Nations to create a plan for the partitioning of Palestine and the creation of a Jewish state.

They will praise You—Lord God-of-Us—all Your creations; and Your pious ones, the just that fulfill Your desires, and Your entire nation, the whole house of Israel, they will thank You with joyous song, and they will bless You, and they will laud You, and they will glorify You, and they will extol You, and they will revere You, and they will sanctify You, and they will make sovereign Your name, our King. Because giving thanks to You is good, and it is pleasant to sing praises toward Your name, for it is from infinity and to infinity that You are God.

Thanks to the Lord for He is good, everlasting is His lovingkindness.
Thanks to the God of gods, everlasting is His lovingkindness.
Thanks to the Master of masters, everlasting is His lovingkindness.
To the sole performer of miraculous wonders, everlasting is His lovingkindness.
To the Maker of the heavens through His insight, everlasting is His lovingkindness.
To the one who spread the earth atop the waters, everlasting is His lovingkindness.
To the Maker of titanic lights, everlasting is His lovingkindness.
The sun, to rule by day, everlasting is His lovingkindness.
The moon and stars, to rule by night, everlasting is His lovingkindness.
To the one who smote Egypt's firstborn, everlasting is His lovingkindness.
And lifted Israel from Egypt's midst, everlasting is His lovingkindness.
In the mighty hand of an outstretched arm, everlasting is His lovingkindness.
To the one who parted the Sea of Reeds, everlasting is His lovingkindness.
And shepherded Israel through it, everlasting is His lovingkindness.
And scattered Pharaoh and his soldiers in the Sea of Reeds, everlasting is His lovingkindness.
To the one who led his nation through the desert, everlasting is His lovingkindness.
To the one who smote great kings, everlasting is His lovingkindness.
And who killed mighty kings, everlasting is His lovingkindness.
— Sihon, King of the Amori, everlasting is His lovingkindness.
— Og, King of the Bashan, everlasting is His lovingkindness.
And gave their land as a dominion, everlasting is His lovingkindness.
A dominion for Israel, His servant, everlasting is His lovingkindness.
And in our nadir remembered us, everlasting is His lovingkindness.
And wrested us from our tormentors, everlasting is His lovingkindness.
He who provides food to all flesh, everlasting is His lovingkindness.
Thanks to the God of heaven, everlasting is His lovingkindness.

1948

In his poem
"In Egypt," the
Holocaust survivor
Paul Celan writes:
"Thou shalt say
to the eye of the
woman stranger: Be
the water.
Thou shalt seek in
the stranger's eye
those thou knowest
are in the water."

נִשְׁמַת כָּל חַי תְּבָרֵךְ אֶת שִׁמְךָ
יהוה אֱלֹהֵינוּ, וְרוּחַ כָּל בָּשָׂר תְּפָאֵר וּתְרוֹמֵם
זִכְרְךָ מַלְכֵּנוּ תָּמִיד. מִן הָעוֹלָם וְעַד הָעוֹלָם אַתָּה אֵל
וּמִבַּלְעָדֶיךָ אֵין לָנוּ מֶלֶךְ גּוֹאֵל וּמוֹשִׁיעַ,
פּוֹדֶה וּמַצִּיל וּמְפַרְנֵס וּמְרַחֵם בְּכָל עֵת
צָרָה וְצוּקָה. אֵין לָנוּ מֶלֶךְ אֶלָּא אָתָּה.
אֱלֹהֵי הָרִאשׁוֹנִים וְהָאַחֲרוֹנִים, אֱלוֹהַּ כָּל בְּרִיּוֹת.
אֲדוֹן כָּל תּוֹלָדוֹת, הַמְהֻלָּל בְּרֹב הַתִּשְׁבָּחוֹת,
הַמְנַהֵג עוֹלָמוֹ בְּחֶסֶד וּבְרִיּוֹתָיו בְּרַחֲמִים. וַיהוה
לֹא יָנוּם וְלֹא יִישָׁן, הַמְעוֹרֵר יְשֵׁנִים,
וְהַמֵּקִיץ נִרְדָּמִים, וְהַמֵּשִׂיחַ אִלְּמִים, וְהַמַּתִּיר
אֲסוּרִים, וְהַסּוֹמֵךְ נוֹפְלִים, וְהַזּוֹקֵף כְּפוּפִים,
לְךָ לְבַדְּךָ אֲנַחְנוּ מוֹדִים.

אִלּוּ פִינוּ מָלֵא שִׁירָה כַּיָּם
וּלְשׁוֹנֵנוּ רִנָּה כַּהֲמוֹן גַּלָּיו
וְשִׂפְתוֹתֵינוּ שֶׁבַח כְּמֶרְחֲבֵי רָקִיעַ
וְעֵינֵינוּ מְאִירוֹת כַּשֶּׁמֶשׁ וְכַיָּרֵחַ
וְיָדֵינוּ פְרוּשׂוֹת כְּנִשְׁרֵי שָׁמָיִם.
וְרַגְלֵינוּ קַלּוֹת כָּאַיָּלוֹת
אֵין אֲנַחְנוּ מַסְפִּיקִים לְהוֹדוֹת לְךָ, יהוה
אֱלֹהֵינוּ וֵאלֹהֵי אֲבוֹתֵינוּ, וּלְבָרֵךְ אֶת שִׁמְךָ עַל
אַחַת מֵאֶלֶף אֶלֶף אַלְפֵי אֲלָפִים וְרִבֵּי רְבָבוֹת
פְּעָמִים הַטּוֹבוֹת שֶׁעָשִׂיתָ עִם אֲבוֹתֵינוּ וְעִמָּנוּ.

מִמִּצְרַיִם גְּאַלְתָּנוּ, יהוה אֱלֹהֵינוּ,
וּמִבֵּית עֲבָדִים פְּדִיתָנוּ, בְּרָעָב זַנְתָּנוּ, וּבְשָׂבָע
כִּלְכַּלְתָּנוּ, מֵחֶרֶב הִצַּלְתָּנוּ, וּמִדֶּבֶר
מִלַּטְתָּנוּ, וּמֵחֳלָיִם רָעִים וְנֶאֱמָנִים דִּלִּיתָנוּ. עַד
הֵנָּה עֲזָרוּנוּ רַחֲמֶיךָ, וְלֹא עֲזָבוּנוּ חֲסָדֶיךָ, וְאַל
תִּטְּשֵׁנוּ, יהוה אֱלֹהֵינוּ, לָנֶצַח. עַל כֵּן, אֵבָרִים

שֶׁפִּלַּגְתָּ בָּנוּ, וְרוּחַ וּנְשָׁמָה שֶׁנָּפַחְתָּ בְּאַפֵּינוּ,
וְלָשׁוֹן אֲשֶׁר שַׂמְתָּ בְּפִינוּ, הֵן הֵם יוֹדוּ וִיבָרְכוּ
וִישַׁבְּחוּ וִיפָאֲרוּ וִירוֹמְמוּ וְיַעֲרִיצוּ וְיַקְדִּישׁוּ
וְיַמְלִיכוּ אֶת שִׁמְךָ מַלְכֵּנוּ, כִּי כָל פֶּה לְךָ יוֹדֶה,
וְכָל לָשׁוֹן לְךָ תִשָּׁבַע, וְכָל בֶּרֶךְ לְךָ תִכְרַע, וְכָל
קוֹמָה לְפָנֶיךָ תִשְׁתַּחֲוֶה, וְכָל לְבָבוֹת יִירָאוּךָ,
וְכָל קֶרֶב וּכְלָיוֹת יְזַמְּרוּ לִשְׁמֶךָ. כַּדָּבָר שֶׁכָּתוּב:
כָּל עַצְמוֹתַי תֹּאמַרְנָה, יהוה מִי כָמוֹךָ, מַצִּיל עָנִי
מֵחָזָק מִמֶּנּוּ, וְעָנִי וְאֶבְיוֹן מִגֹּזְלוֹ. מִי יִדְמֶה
לָךְ וּמִי יִשְׁוֶה לָּךְ וּמִי יַעֲרָךְ לָךְ, הָאֵל הַגָּדוֹל
הַגִּבּוֹר וְהַנּוֹרָא, אֵל עֶלְיוֹן, קֹנֵה שָׁמַיִם וָאָרֶץ.
נְהַלֶּלְךָ וּנְשַׁבֵּחֲךָ וּנְפָאֶרְךָ וּנְבָרֵךְ אֶת שֵׁם
קָדְשֶׁךָ, כָּאָמוּר: לְדָוִד. בָּרְכִי נַפְשִׁי אֶת יהוה,
וְכָל קְרָבַי אֶת שֵׁם קָדְשׁוֹ.

every belly and its innards will sing Your
name. As it is written: All of my bones
will exclaim, Lord, who is like You, who
rescues the poor man from the one more
powerful, and the poor and pauper from
the one who preys upon them. Who could
compare to You, and who could be equal
to You, and who could measure to You in
value, the God monumental, the mighty
and awesome, God supreme, Proprietor of
the heavens and the earth. We will praise
you, and we will laud You, and we will
glorify You, and we will bless Your holy
name, as it is said: *By David. My soul does
bless the Lord, and all I contain blesses His
holy name.*

1950

The world's Jewish population is approximately 11.7 million, or about 0.5% of the total global population. In the wake of the Holocaust, Europe's share of the global Jewish population drops to 30.9%, while half of the world's remaining Jews live in the Americas.

1949

On September 4, the African-American scholar, athlete, actor, and singer Paul Robeson performs "Go Down, Moses" during a concert in Peekskill, New York. Because of Robeson's leftist politics, a mob attacks concertgoers after the performance, injuring 145 people.

Let the spirit of all life bless Your name, Lord God-of-Us, and the breath of all flesh glorify and extol our remembrance of You, our eternal King. From infinity and to infinity You are God, and without You we have no King to redeem and deliver, to ransom and rescue, to provide and be compassionate through every period of difficulty and distress. We have no King but You—God of the first and the last, God of all creations, Master of all generations, who is praised with an abundance of veneration, who pilots His world with beneficence and His creations with compassion. And the Lord does not drowse and does not sleep; He is the one who wakes sleepers and rouses those under the spell of slumber, who gives voice to the mute, and unbinds the bound, and braces the falling, and straightens the bent. It is to You—to You alone—that we are thankful.

Were our mouths filled with a singing like the sea, and our tongues awash with song, as waves countless, and our lips lauding, as the skies are wide, and our eyes illumined like the sun and the moon, and our hands spread out like the eagles of heaven, and our feet as fleet as fawns—still, we would not suffice in thanking You, Lord God-of-Us, and God of our fathers, in blessing Your name for even one of a thousand thousand, from the thousands of thousands, and the ten thousands of ten thousands of times you did good turns for our fathers and for us.

From Egypt You delivered us, Lord God-of-Us, and from the house of servitude You ransomed us. In hunger You nourished, in plenty You provided, from the sword You rescued, from pestilence You let us slip away, and from disease—evil and enduring—You drew us. Until this point, we were aided by Your compassion, Your lovingkindness never left us—and do not abandon us, Lord God-of-Us, for eternity. And so, the limbs that you apportioned us, and the spirit and the soul that you breathed into our nostrils, and the tongue that You placed in our mouths—they will thank You, and they will bless You, and they will laud You, and they will glorify You, and they will extol You, and they will revere You, and they will sanctify You, and they will make sovereign Your name, our King. Because every mouth, to You will thank, and every tongue, to You will pledge, and every knee, to You will kneel, and all who stand, to You will bow flat out, and all hearts will be in awe of You, and

1951

Israel completes
what it calls
Operation Ezra and
Nehemiah, which
brings 120,000 Iraqi
Jews—nearly all of
the country's Jewish
population—to Israel.
While a few remain,
the operation
effectively ends
2,000 years of
Jewish communal life
in Iraq.

הָאֵל בְּתַעֲצֻמוֹת עֻזֶּךָ, הַגָּדוֹל בִּכְבוֹד
שְׁמֶךָ, הַגִּבּוֹר לָנֶצַח וְהַנּוֹרָא בְּנוֹרְאוֹתֶיךָ, הַמֶּלֶךְ
הַיּוֹשֵׁב עַל כִּסֵּא רָם וְנִשָּׂא.

שׁוֹכֵן עַד, מָרוֹם וְקָדוֹשׁ שְׁמוֹ. וְכָתוּב:
רַנְּנוּ צַדִּיקִים בַּיהוה, לַיְשָׁרִים נָאוָה תְהִלָּה.
בְּפִי יְשָׁרִים תִּתְהַלָּל, וּבְדִבְרֵי צַדִּיקִים תִּתְבָּרַךְ,
וּבִלְשׁוֹן חֲסִידִים תִּתְרוֹמָם, וּבְקֶרֶב
קְדוֹשִׁים תִּתְקַדָּשׁ.

וּבְמַקְהֲלוֹת רִבְבוֹת עַמְּךָ בֵּית יִשְׂרָאֵל, בְּרִנָּה
יִתְפָּאַר שִׁמְךָ מַלְכֵּנוּ בְּכָל דּוֹר וָדוֹר. שֶׁכֵּן
חוֹבַת כָּל הַיְצוּרִים לְפָנֶיךָ, יהוה אֱלֹהֵינוּ וֵאלֹהֵי
אֲבוֹתֵינוּ, לְהוֹדוֹת לְהַלֵּל לְשַׁבֵּחַ לְפָאֵר
לְרוֹמֵם לְהַדֵּר לְבָרֵךְ לְעַלֵּה וּלְקַלֵּס עַל
כָּל דִּבְרֵי שִׁירוֹת וְתִשְׁבְּחוֹת דָּוִד בֶּן יִשַׁי
עַבְדְּךָ מְשִׁיחֶךָ.

יִשְׁתַּבַּח שִׁמְךָ לָעַד מַלְכֵּנוּ, הָאֵל הַמֶּלֶךְ
הַגָּדוֹל וְהַקָּדוֹשׁ בַּשָּׁמַיִם וּבָאָרֶץ. כִּי לְךָ נָאֶה,
יהוה אֱלֹהֵינוּ וֵאלֹהֵי אֲבוֹתֵינוּ, שִׁיר וּשְׁבָחָה,
הַלֵּל וְזִמְרָה, עֹז וּמֶמְשָׁלָה, נֶצַח, גְּדֻלָּה
וּגְבוּרָה, תְּהִלָּה וְתִפְאֶרֶת, קְדֻשָּׁה וּמַלְכוּת,
בְּרָכוֹת וְהוֹדָאוֹת מֵעַתָּה וְעַד עוֹלָם. בָּרוּךְ
אַתָּה יהוה, אֵל מֶלֶךְ גָּדוֹל בַּתִּשְׁבָּחוֹת,
אֵל הַהוֹדָאוֹת, אֲדוֹן הַנִּפְלָאוֹת, הַבּוֹחֵר בְּשִׁירֵי
זִמְרָה, מֶלֶךְ, אֵל, חֵי הָעוֹלָמִים.

1952

The first page of the official Haggadah of the United States Armed Forces features Benjamin Franklin's 1776 proposal for the Seal of the United States.

1951

The Viennese-born composer Arnold Schönberg dies in Los Angeles, leaving unfinished his twelve-tone opera *Moses und Aron*, a musical interpretation of the Exodus that offers not heroics but a meditation on the flaws, struggles, and limitations of the Jewish leaders.

God—by Your ultimate strength; Great—by the honor of Your name; Mighty—eternally; Awesome—in Your terrible awesomeness; the King who sits on a throne most lofty and raised.

He who dwells eternal, towering and sanctified is His name. And it is written: *Rejoice, righteous ones, in the Lord, to the just, praise is beauty.* By the mouths of the upright You will be praised, and by the words of the righteous You will be blessed, and by the talk of the pious You will be uplifted, and amidst the sanctified You will be sanctified.

Great crowds of Your nation, the house of Israel, will gather. In generation after generation, they will join in joyous song to glorify Your name, our King.

For this is the obligation of all creation before You, Lord God-of-Us and God of our fathers, to give thanks, to sing praise, to venerate, to glorify, to exalt, to beautify, to bless, to uplift and applaud, even beyond all the words of the songs and praises of David, son of Ishai, Your servant, Your anointed one.

Your name be praised forever, God, our King, great and holy ruler of heaven and earth. For to You—Lord God-of-Us and God of our fathers—it is befitting: song and praise, praise in song and melody, might and dominion, eternal victory, greatness and strength, thanksgiving and glory, sanctification and sovereignty, blessings and thanks, from now until forever. You are blessed Lord, God, King preeminent in praises, God of our thanks, master of wonders, who chooses melodious songs, King, God, life of the universe.

Cecil B. DeMille
releases his
Technicolor epic *The
Ten Commandments*,
billed as "the
Greatest Event in
Motion Picture
History." As the
on-screen Israelites
prepare to flee
Egypt, Moses' son
Gershom asks, "Why
is this night different
from all others?"
Moses replies,
"Because this night
the Lord our God will
deliver us from the
bondage of Egypt."

כוס רביעי

הִנְנִי מוּכָן/מוּכָנָה וּמְזֻמָּן/וּמְזֻמֶּנֶת לְקַיֵּם
מִצְוַת כּוֹס רְבִיעִי שֶׁהוּא כְּנֶגֶד בְּשׂוֹרַת
הַיְשׁוּעָה שֶׁאָמַר הַקָּדוֹשׁ בָּרוּךְ הוּא
לְיִשְׂרָאֵל: וְלָקַחְתִּי אֶתְכֶם לִי לְעָם
וְהָיִיתִי לָכֶם לֵאלֹהִים.

בָּרוּךְ אַתָּה יהוה, אֱלֹהֵינוּ מֶלֶךְ הָעוֹלָם,
בּוֹרֵא פְּרִי הַגָּפֶן.

בָּרוּךְ אַתָּה יהוה, אֱלֹהֵינוּ מֶלֶךְ הָעוֹלָם,
עַל הַגֶּפֶן וְעַל פְּרִי הַגֶּפֶן, וְעַל תְּנוּבַת
הַשָּׂדֶה, וְעַל אֶרֶץ חֶמְדָּה טוֹבָה וּרְחָבָה,

שֶׁרָצִיתָ וְהִנְחַלְתָּ לַאֲבוֹתֵינוּ לֶאֱכוֹל מִפִּרְיָהּ
וְלִשְׂבּוֹעַ מִטּוּבָהּ. רַחֶם נָא יהוה אֱלֹהֵינוּ
עַל יִשְׂרָאֵל עַמֶּךָ, וְעַל יְרוּשָׁלַיִם עִירֶךָ, וְעַל
צִיּוֹן מִשְׁכַּן כְּבוֹדֶךָ וְעַל מִזְבְּחֶךָ וְעַל הֵיכָלֶךָ.
וּבְנֵה יְרוּשָׁלַיִם עִיר הַקֹּדֶשׁ בִּמְהֵרָה
בְיָמֵינוּ, וְהַעֲלֵנוּ לְתוֹכָהּ וְשַׂמְּחֵנוּ
בְּבִנְיָנָהּ, וְנֹאכַל מִפִּרְיָהּ וְנִשְׂבַּע מִטּוּבָהּ
וּנְבָרֶכְךָ עָלֶיהָ בִּקְדֻשָׁה וּבְטָהֳרָה. [וּרְצֵה
וְהַחֲלִיצֵנוּ בְּיוֹם הַשַּׁבָּת הַזֶּה] וְשַׂמְּחֵנוּ בְּיוֹם
חַג הַמַּצּוֹת הַזֶּה, כִּי אַתָּה יהוה טוֹב וּמֵטִיב
לַכֹּל, וְנוֹדֶה לְּךָ עַל הָאָרֶץ וְעַל פְּרִי הַגָּפֶן. בָּרוּךְ
אַתָּה יהוה, עַל הָאָרֶץ וְעַל פְּרִי הַגָּפֶן.

1957

For the first time, the United States is home to the world's largest number of Jews—43% of the global Jewish population and 3.1% of the total population of the United States.

Fourth Cup

Raise the cup of wine and recite:

Here I am, prepared and ardent, allied and present, ready to perform the mitzvah of the fourth cup, the enactment of salvation's promise. As the Holy One, Blessed is He, declared to Israel: *And I will take you for myself as a nation, and I will be for you as a God.*

You are blessed, Lord God-of-Us, King of the Cosmos, Maker of the fruit of the vine.

While reclining, drink at least most of the cup. When finished, recite (on Shabbat, add the words in brackets):

You are blessed, Lord God-of-Us, King of the Cosmos, for the vines, and for the fruit of the vine, for the bounty of the fields, and for the sweet, rich, broad ground that you found favorable, and bequeathed to our fathers, letting them eat from her fruit and be sated on her excellence. Mercy, please—Lord God-of-Us—on Israel Your nation, on Jerusalem Your city, on Zion the dwelling place of Your honor, on Your altar and on Your temple. And may You rebuild Jerusalem, the holy city, with speed and in our days, and usher us up into it, and see us rejoice in its renewal. We will eat from her fruits, and be sated on her excellence, and we will bless You for all of it, in sanctity and in purity. [Find favor and fortify us, on this day of Shabbat.] See us rejoice on the day of this Festival of Matzot, because You, Lord, are good, and make good for all, and we thank You for the land and for the fruit of the vine. You are blessed, Lord, for the land and for the fruit of the vine.

נִרְצָה

חֲסַל סִדּוּר פֶּסַח כְּהִלְכָתוֹ,
כְּכָל מִשְׁפָּטוֹ וְחֻקָתוֹ.
כַּאֲשֶׁר זָכִינוּ לְסַדֵּר אוֹתוֹ,
כֵּן נִזְכֶּה לַעֲשׂוֹתוֹ.
זָךְ שׁוֹכֵן מְעוֹנָה,
קוֹמֵם קְהַל עֲדַת מִי מָנָה.
בְּקָרוֹב נַהֵל נִטְעֵי כַנָּה,
פְּדוּיִם לְצִיּוֹן בְּרִנָּה.

Nirzah

Here concludes the Passover seder, in accordance with its rules, all its laws and dictums.

Just as we were fortunate enough to make this seder, so may we be fortunate enough to do it again.

Pure One who dwells on high, raise up a community, a people beyond counting.

May You soon guide those sturdy stems, those freed people, on to Zion with songs of joy.

Say out loud: # Next year in Jerusalem!

לְשָׁנָה הַבָּאָה בִּירוּשָׁלַיִם...

The Haggadah saves the most demanding call for the

final moment of the seder. "Next year in Jerusalem," we declare, sometimes nervously, sometimes self-consciously, often ambivalently. Think about it: We can achieve in less than a day what it took our ancestors forty years to do—move to Israel and become citizens of a Jewish state. This call was, for most of the Passovers of Jewish history, a messianic aspiration; Jerusalem was an unachievable goal. Things have changed. Zionism, the most successful national liberation movement of the twentieth century, has made it possible for us to do what Moses could not.

And yet: Does "Next year in Jerusalem" mean that we are actually supposed to make aliyah, tomorrow? The comfortable answer is: *No, obviously not.* The uncomfortable answer is: *Yes.* Imagine having the ability to commune with your distant and downtrodden ancestors, in their scattered shtetls and ghettos. You happily inform them that, yes, for the first time since the Romans ethnically cleansed Israel, a Jewish state exists. They are overwhelmed with joy and ask, "What is it like to live there?" And you answer, "Well, I wouldn't actually know."

At the very least, we can understand the call "Next year in Jerusalem" as a repudiation of the wicked son: Jews, no matter our politics, have a special responsibility to tie ourselves to Israel's fate, and to work for the vision of Israel in which we believe. But "Next year in Jerusalem" also has a spiritual meaning. In Jerusalem itself, the seder concludes with the call "Next year in *rebuilt* Jerusalem."

The Jerusalem Jerusalemites are striving for is something else altogether, the Jerusalem on high. Jerusalem is the symbol of peace, the destination of the Messiah, the holiest place on earth, the purest expression of the profound Jewish belief that the world will one day be a better place. It is this idea of Jerusalem for which we also reach. When we reach it—and we will, for that is the core Jewish belief—there will be no more need for seders and Haggadot: We will live in a world in which the poor are fed and sheltered and the sick healed; in which the Jews are accepted as a free people; in which no one is persecuted or enslaved. Until that day arrives, we will continue to gather around the Passover table, to remind ourselves, and each other, of the work we must do. So, what are you going to do?

Nation

It is very likely that you are reading

this in the Diaspora, a word which here means "everywhere in the universe except Israel." Even though Israel is designated as the Jewish homeland, most Jews live in the Diaspora, for any number of good or bad reasons. Whatever your reasons are for living in the Diaspora, to some extent Israel is still your home tonight, for when you read the story of Passover and think about the journey from slavery to freedom, you accompany those Jewish slaves on that journey, and part of their struggle stays with you, the way the heroes of any good story stay with you long after you are done reading. Their journey ends in Jerusalem, a place of freedom and safety for the Jewish people, and so we end the seder with the words "Next year in Jerusalem," acknowledging their longing for a home and their satisfaction at finally finding one. Even if you do not believe you will celebrate Passover next year in Jerusalem, you may say these words and think of your own home, which I hope is one of freedom and safety, and the journeys of all the people in the world, which are often difficult and treacherous, as they try to find homes for themselves. Next year, we hope everyone in the world has freedom and safety and can celebrate holidays in a home full of fellow travelers who wish them well, just as everyone at your Passover table wishes you well, even the person you like the least. Let us be grateful for the homes we have, and hopeful for the homes of others, this year in the Diaspora, and next year in Jerusalem.

Playground

Next Year in Jerusalem

The seder ends in an outburst of longing, and it is a longing for home. No matter where we are, the chances are that we feel displaced. No strangers to estrangement, we carry a homesickness from place to place.

Library

Somewhere on earth will feel like home. We will know it down to its homeliest details, and that knowledge will seep through and calm our restlessness, for what was that restlessness but a dream of coming home?

Next year in Jerusalem! we sing, from our places scattered around the globe, including the city of Jerusalem itself. And we will sing it year after year, no matter how history disposes of us, just so long as we are still around. Proust wrote, "There is no paradise but paradise lost." The Jerusalem with which we end the seder is a place in the Proustian dreamscape, only designated not by the ache of loss but the ache of longing.

And if Jerusalem is metaphor, so, too, is Egypt. Egypt is the here and now, using the most persuasive of means—the fact of reality itself—to make us sink into its presence and forget the boundaries we had meant to cross.

The Haggadah's tale is about a family who swell into something more. Voluntary strangers, they became involuntary slaves and finally head out into the unknown, driven by their longing to go home. None of them would ever reach that home, not even Moses.

Next year in Jerusalem, we say, and the words send us out into the night with our desires stoked, our contentment cooled.

We are slaves without our longings.

House of Study

We live in a broken world... Exile—another name for brokenness—is not just the current condition of the Jewish people, according to the Kabbalah, it is the fundamental condition of the universe and of God. Before the Beginning, before there was a heaven and an earth, God's light poured forth, intended for divine vessels. But the vessels were not strong enough to hold the light and, in a primordial catastrophe known as "the shattering of the vessels" (shevirat ha-kelim), the divine light—God's very being—was scattered like so many sparks. Today, we live surrounded by these sparks and the shards of the vessels that were meant to hold them.

But there is one place in this broken world whose very name contains the Hebrew word—shalem—for wholeness, peace, and perfection. That place is Jerusalem. The rabbis teach us that Jerusalem marks the spot where God laid the foundation stone (even ha-shetiya) upon which he created the rest of the world. For this reason, they call Jerusalem the "navel of the world" (tabbur ha'aretz) and the "gateway to heaven" (sha'ar ha-shamayim).

When we sing "Next year in Jerusalem," therefore, we are asking for a new beginning; for a return to wholeness.

And yet...

And yet, there is another Jewish tradition, this time from Hasidism, that teaches us the virtue, even the necessity of "being broken" (tsubrokhenkayt). As a Hasidic saying paradoxically declares: "There is nothing more whole than a broken heart." Ayn davar yoter shalem me lev shavur. Here, again, we find the same Hebrew word for "whole"— shalem—that lies at the root of Jerusalem.

So what is the wholeness that we seek when we sing "Next year in Jerusalem"? Is it a return from exile or the embrace of a broken heart? Is exile a punishment that distances us from God or an opportunity to get closer to him? Is it more Jewish to be broken than whole? Or is the point of Judaism the attempt to find wholeness in brokenness?

1959

At 30 West 68th Street in New York City, the Stephen Wise Free Synagogue holds an interfaith and interracial seder, based on the principle of "freedom as every man's birthright as a child of God."

וּבְכֵן וַיְהִי בַּחֲצִי הַלַּיְלָה

אָז רֹוב נִסִּים הִפְלֵאתָ   בַּלַּיְלָה.
בְּרֹאשׁ אַשְׁמֹורֶת זֶה   הַלַּיְלָה.
גֵּר צֶדֶק נִצַּחְתֹּו כְּנֶחֱלַק לֹו   לַיְלָה.

וַיְהִי בַּחֲצִי הַלַּיְלָה.

דַּנְתָּ מֶלֶךְ גְּרָר בַּחֲלֹום   הַלַּיְלָה.
הִפְחַדְתָּ אֲרַמִּי בְּאֶמֶשׁ   לַיְלָה.
וַיָּשַׂר יִשְׂרָאֵל לְמַלְאָךְ וַיּוּכַל לֹו   לַיְלָה.

וַיְהִי בַּחֲצִי הַלַּיְלָה.

זֶרַע בְּכֹורֵי פַתְרֹוס מָחַצְתָּ בַּחֲצִי   הַלַּיְלָה.
חֵילָם לֹא מָצְאוּ בְּקוּמָם   בַּלַּיְלָה.
טִיסַת נְגִיד חֲרֹשֶׁת סִלִּיתָ בְּכֹוכְבֵי   לַיְלָה.

וַיְהִי בַּחֲצִי הַלַּיְלָה.

יָעַץ מְחָרֵף לְנֹופֵף אִוּוּי הֹובַשְׁתָּ פְגָרָיו   בַּלַּיְלָה.
כָּרַע בֵּל וּמַצָּבֹו בְּאִישֹׁון   לַיְלָה.
לְאִישׁ חֲמוּדֹות נִגְלָה רָז חֲזֹות   לַיְלָה.

וַיְהִי בַּחֲצִי הַלַּיְלָה.

מִשְׁתַּכֵּר בִּכְלֵי קֹדֶשׁ נֶהֱרַג בֹּו   בַּלַּיְלָה.
נֹושַׁע מִבֹּור אֲרָיֹות פֹּותֵר בִּעֲתוּתֵי   לַיְלָה.
שִׂנְאָה נָטַר אֲגָגִי וְכָתַב סְפָרִים   בַּלַּיְלָה.

וַיְהִי בַּחֲצִי הַלַּיְלָה.

עֹורַרְתָּ נִצְחֲךָ עָלָיו בְּנֶדֶד שְׁנַת   לַיְלָה.
פּוּרָה תִדְרֹוךְ לְשֹׁמֵר מַה   מִלַּיְלָה.
צָרַח כַּשֹּׁומֵר וְשָׂח אָתָא בֹקֶר וְגַם   לַיְלָה.

וַיְהִי בַּחֲצִי הַלַּיְלָה.

קָרֵב יֹום אֲשֶׁר הוּא לֹא יֹום וְלֹא   לַיְלָה.
רָם הֹודַע כִּי לְךָ הַיֹּום אַף לְךָ   הַלַּיְלָה.
שֹׁומְרִים הַפְקֵד לְעִירְךָ כָּל הַיֹּום וְכָל   הַלַּיְלָה.
תָּאִיר כְּאֹור יֹום חֶשְׁכַּת   לַיְלָה.

וַיְהִי בַּחֲצִי הַלַּיְלָה.

Recruit for Your city watchmen,
for all the day and all   the night.
Illumine as if the light of day,
the dark of   night.

And so it was at midnight.

One day before his assassination, the Rev. Martin Luther King Jr. speaks in Memphis, Tennessee: "If I were standing at the beginning of time... and the Almighty said to me, 'Martin Luther King, which age would you like to live in?' I would take my mental flight by Egypt and I would watch God's children in their magnificent trek from the dark dungeons of Egypt...across the Red Sea, through the wilderness on toward the promised land.... The cry is always the same— 'We want to be free.'"

Chant this hymn on the first seder night only.

And thus, so it was at midnight.

With many miracles you mesmerized	at night.	You toppled Bel and its monument	
At the start of first watch on	this night.	in the thick of	night.
You aided the righteous convert in		To the one adored, the vision's secret	
conquest when was split for him—	night.	was revealed of a	night.

And so it was at midnight—   **And so it was at midnight—**

You took the King of Grar to task in		Got himself drunk using the holy vessels	
a dream	this night.	and on that day he was killed	at night.
You put fear into an Aramean in		Delivered from the lion's den,	
the gloom of	night.	he interprets the terrors of	night.
And Israel wrestled with an Angel and		The Agagi bore hatred,	
prevailed of a	night.	penning his polemics	at night.

And so it was at midnight—   **And so it was at midnight—**

The firstborn offspring of Patros,		You awoke Your victory over him	
You clove in the middle of	this night.	by disturbing the sleep of	night.
They did not find their strength		You will stomp in the winepress for	
when stirring	at night.	those who ask the watchman, What	of the night?
The Prince of Haroshet took flight,		Roar like a watchman, and declare,	
trampled by the orbiting stars of	night.	Morning is coming as well as	night.

And so it was at midnight—   **And so it was at midnight—**

The blasphemer conspired against Your		Usher in a day that is not day and is not	night.
dwelling of desire, You humiliated him		Make known, Exalted, that to You	
with corpses	at night.	belongs the day and also to You	the night.

On the first anniversary of King's death, in the basement of a black church in Washington, DC, Rabbi Arthur Waskow holds a "Freedom Seder" for 800 people, half of them Jews and half black and white Christians, with the blessing: "Blessed art thou, O Lord, who hast made all peoples holy and hast commanded us, even against our will, to become a beacon for justice and freedom for them all." The service becomes the inspiration for Freedom Seders that place the link between the Exodus story and modern political struggles at the center of the ritual.

וּבְכֵן וַאֲמַרְתֶּם זֶבַח פֶּסַח

פֶּסַח.	מִסְגֶּרֶת סֻגְּרָה בְּעִתּוֹתֵי	בְּפֶסַח. אֹמֶץ גְּבוּרוֹתֶיךָ הִפְלֵאתָ
פֶּסַח.	נִשְׁמְדָה מִדְיָן בִּצְלִיל שְׂעוֹרֵי עֹמֶר	פֶּסַח. בְּרֹאשׁ כָּל מוֹעֲדוֹת נִשֵּׂאתָ
פֶּסַח.	שֹׂרְפוּ מִשְׁמַנֵּי פּוּל וְלוּד בִּיקַד יְקוֹד	פֶּסַח. גִּלִּיתָ לְאֶזְרָחִי חֲצוֹת לֵיל

וַאֲמַרְתֶּם זֶבַח פֶּסַח

וַאֲמַרְתֶּם זֶבַח פֶּסַח

פֶּסַח	עוֹד הַיּוֹם בְּנֹב לַעֲמוֹד עַד גָּעָה עוֹנַת	בְּפֶסַח. דְּלָתָיו דָּפַקְתָּ כְּחֹם הַיּוֹם
בְּפֶסַח.	פַּס יַד כָּתְבָה לְקַעֲקֵעַ צוּל	בְּפֶסַח. הִסְעִיד נוֹצְצִים עֻגוֹת מַצּוֹת
בְּפֶסַח.	צָפֹה הַצָּפִית עָרוֹךְ הַשֻּׁלְחָן	פֶּסַח. וְאֶל הַבָּקָר רָץ זֵכֶר לְשׁוֹר עֵרֶךְ

וַאֲמַרְתֶּם זֶבַח פֶּסַח

וַאֲמַרְתֶּם זֶבַח פֶּסַח

בְּפֶסַח.	קָהָל כִּנְּסָה הֲדַסָּה צוֹם לְשַׁלֵּשׁ	בְּפֶסַח. זֹעֲמוּ סְדוֹמִים וְלֹהֲטוּ בָּאֵשׁ
בְּפֶסַח.	רֹאשׁ מִבֵּית רָשָׁע מָחַצְתָּ בְּעֵץ חֲמִשִּׁים	פֶּסַח. חֻלַּץ לוֹט מֵהֶם וּמַצּוֹת אָפָה בְּקֵץ
בְּפֶסַח.	שְׁתֵּי אֵלֶּה רֶגַע תָּבִיא לְעוּצִית	בְּפֶסַח. טִאטֵאתָ אַדְמַת מוֹף וְנוֹף בְּעָבְרְךָ
	תָּעֹז יָדְךָ וְתָרוּם יְמִינְךָ כְּלֵיל הִתְקַדֶּשׁ חַג	

וַאֲמַרְתֶּם זֶבַח פֶּסַח

וַאֲמַרְתֶּם זֶבַח פֶּסַח

פֶּסַח.	יָהּ רֹאשׁ כָּל אוֹן מָחַצְתָּ בְּלֵיל שִׁמּוּר
פֶּסַח.	כַּבִּיר עַל בֵּן בְּכוֹר פָּסַחְתָּ בְּדַם
בְּפֶסַח.	לְבִלְתִּי תֵּת מַשְׁחִית לָבֹא בִּפְתָחַי

וַאֲמַרְתֶּם זֶבַח פֶּסַח

And proclaim, This is the Passover sacrifice.

Hadassah gathered the congregation to fast for three days	on Pesach.
You broke the head of a wicked household on the fifty-cubit tree	on Pesach.
You will simultaneously deliver these two things upon the Utzites	on Pesach.
Your hand be mighty, Your right arm rise up, as on the night You made holy the holiday	Pesach.

And proclaim, This is the Passover sacrifice.

1972

In Brooklyn, a women's collective creates the first feminist Haggadah. In the late 1980s, some seders include an additional cup of wine to honor Miriam as well as Elijah. Some begin to add an orange to their seder plates, precisely because it seems out of place, in order to recognize and welcome all those who are marginalized within the Jewish community, particularly lesbians and gay men.

Chant this hymn on the second seder night only.

And therefore, proclaim, This is the Passover sacrifice.

With the might of Your might You mesmerized	on Pesach.
Above the heads of all holidays, You raised up	Pesach.
You revealed to the native-born one the promise of the midnight of	Pesach.

And proclaim, This is the Passover sacrifice.

You knocked upon his door during the heat of the day	on Pesach.
He served the sparkling ones cakes of matzah	on Pesach.
And he ran to the cattle—a reminder to us of the ideal sacrificial ox of	Pesach.

And proclaim, This is the Passover sacrifice.

The Sodomites were enraged, and were engulfed by fire	on Pesach.
Lot was delivered from among them, and baked matzah at the end of	Pesach.
You swept clean the Egyptian lands of Moph and Noph when you passed over	on Pesach.

And proclaim, This is the Passover sacrifice.

God, You ground down the heads of their virility during the protected night of	Pesach.
Mighty One, You passed above the firstborn because of the blood of	Pesach.
So as not to let destruction through my doors	on Pesach.

And proclaim, This is the Passover sacrifice.

The ramparted city surrounded, surrendered in the season of	Pesach.
Midion was annihilated by the rolling barley cake of	Pesach.
The elite of Pul and Lud were incinerated with the flaming fire of	Pesach.

And proclaim, This is the Passover sacrifice.

He waited that day at Nob until the arrival of the season of	Pesach.
By the tip of your hand was written, *Gouge out the depths of Tzul*	*on Pesach.*
The watchman watched, the table was set	on Pesach.

In his 1977 song "Exodus," the Rastafarian musician Bob Marley pleads: "Send us another brother Moses/From across the Red Sea." "Exodus" becomes an international hit, and in 1999, *Time* magazine names *Exodus* the best album of the 20th century.

כִּי לוֹ נָאֶה. כִּי לוֹ יָאֶה.

אַדִּיר בִּמְלוּכָה, בָּחוּר כַּהֲלָכָה,
גְּדוּדָיו יֹאמְרוּ לוֹ:
לְךָ וּלְךָ, לְךָ כִּי לְךָ, לְךָ אַף לְךָ,
לְךָ יְיָ הַמַּמְלָכָה.
כִּי לוֹ נָאֶה. כִּי לוֹ יָאֶה.

מוֹשֵׁל בִּמְלוּכָה, נוֹרָא כַּהֲלָכָה,
סְבִיבָיו יֹאמְרוּ לוֹ:
לְךָ וּלְךָ, לְךָ כִּי לְךָ, לְךָ אַף לְךָ,
לְךָ יְיָ הַמַּמְלָכָה.
כִּי לוֹ נָאֶה. כִּי לוֹ יָאֶה.

דָּגוּל בִּמְלוּכָה, הָדוּר כַּהֲלָכָה,
וָתִיקָיו יֹאמְרוּ לוֹ:
לְךָ וּלְךָ, לְךָ כִּי לְךָ, לְךָ אַף לְךָ,
לְךָ יְיָ הַמַּמְלָכָה.
כִּי לוֹ נָאֶה. כִּי לוֹ יָאֶה.

עָנָיו בִּמְלוּכָה, פּוֹדֶה כַּהֲלָכָה,
צַדִּיקָיו יֹאמְרוּ לוֹ:
לְךָ וּלְךָ, לְךָ כִּי לְךָ, לְךָ אַף לְךָ,
לְךָ יְיָ הַמַּמְלָכָה.
כִּי לוֹ נָאֶה. כִּי לוֹ יָאֶה.

זַכַּאי בִּמְלוּכָה, חָסִין כַּהֲלָכָה,
טַפְסְרָיו יֹאמְרוּ לוֹ:
לְךָ וּלְךָ, לְךָ כִּי לְךָ, לְךָ אַף לְךָ,
לְךָ יְיָ הַמַּמְלָכָה.
כִּי לוֹ נָאֶה. כִּי לוֹ יָאֶה.

קָדוֹשׁ בִּמְלוּכָה, רַחוּם כַּהֲלָכָה,
שִׁנְאַנָּיו יֹאמְרוּ לוֹ:
לְךָ וּלְךָ, לְךָ כִּי לְךָ, לְךָ אַף לְךָ,
לְךָ יְיָ הַמַּמְלָכָה.
כִּי לוֹ נָאֶה. כִּי לוֹ יָאֶה.

יָחִיד בִּמְלוּכָה, כַּבִּיר כַּהֲלָכָה,
לִמּוּדָיו יֹאמְרוּ לוֹ:
לְךָ וּלְךָ, לְךָ כִּי לְךָ, לְךָ אַף לְךָ,
לְךָ יְיָ הַמַּמְלָכָה.
כִּי לוֹ נָאֶה. כִּי לוֹ יָאֶה.

תַּקִּיף בִּמְלוּכָה, תּוֹמֵךְ כַּהֲלָכָה,
תְּמִימָיו יֹאמְרוּ לוֹ:
לְךָ וּלְךָ, לְךָ כִּי לְךָ, לְךָ אַף לְךָ,
לְךָ יְיָ הַמַּמְלָכָה.
כִּי לוֹ נָאֶה. כִּי לוֹ יָאֶה.

The Palestinian literary and cultural critic Edward Said muses on exile: "Most people are principally aware of one culture, one setting, one home; exiles are aware of at least two, and this plurality of vision gives rise to an awareness of simultaneous dimensions, an awareness that—to borrow a phrase from music—is contrapuntal. For an exile, habits of life, expression, or activity in the new environment inevitably occur against the memory of these things in another environment. Thus both the new and the old environments are vivid, actual, occurring together contrapuntally.... There is a unique pleasure in this sort of apprehension."

On both nights, continue:

For to Him it is befitting, for to Him it is befit.

Almighty in His majesty, ideal—as it is supposed to be; His heavenly battalions say to Him: To-You-and-to-You, to-You-for-to-You, to-You-yea-to-You, to-You-Lord-the-kingdom. For to Him it is befitting, for to Him it is befit.

Noble in His majesty, magnificent—as it is supposed to be; His loyalists say to Him: To-You-and-to-You, to-You-for-to-You, to-You-yea-to-You, to-You-Lord-the-kingdom. For to Him it is befitting, for to Him it is befit.

Pristine in His majesty, powerful—as it is supposed to be; His marshals say to Him: To-You-and-to-You, to-You-for-to-You, to-You-yea-to-You, to-You-Lord-the-kingdom. For to Him it is befitting, for to Him it is befit.

Unrivaled in His majesty, omnipotent—as it is supposed to be; His disciples say to Him: To-You-and-to-You, to-You-for-to-You, to-You-yea-to-You, to-You-Lord-the-kingdom. For to Him it is befitting, for to Him it is befit.

Commanding in his majesty, awesome—as it is supposed to be; His inner circle says to Him: To-You-and-to-You, to-You-for-to-You, to-You-yea-to-You, to-You-Lord-the-kingdom. For to Him it is befitting, for to Him it is befit.

Modest in His majesty, redeeming—as it is supposed to be; His righteous say to Him: To-You-and-to-You, to-You-for-to-You, to-You-yea-to-You, to-You-Lord-the-kingdom. For to Him it is befitting, for to Him it is befit.

Sanctified in His majesty, compassionate—as it is supposed to be; His incalculable say to Him: To-You-and-to-You, to-You-for-to-You, to-You-yea-to-You, to-You-Lord-the-kingdom. For to Him it is befitting, for to Him it is befit.

Solid in His majesty, reliant—as it is supposed to be; His wholesome say to Him: To-You-and-to-You, to-You-for-to-You, to-You-yea-to-You, to-You-Lord-the-kingdom. For to Him it is befitting, for to Him it is befit.

The Egyptian-born French-Jewish writer Edmond Jabès writes of the wandering in the desert: "Hidden language, not that of hands or eyes, a language beyond gesture, beyond looks, smiles or tears that we had to learn! Ah, what desert will revive it now? We thought we were done with crossing the desolate stretch of land where the word had dragged us, making us and our wanderings bear amazed witness to its perennial nature. And here silence leads us into its glass kingdom, vaster yet at first sight, breaking all traces of our passage....Write, write, write in order to remember."

אַדִּיר הוּא, יִבְנֶה בֵּיתוֹ בְּקָרוֹב, בִּמְהֵרָה בִּמְהֵרָה, בְּיָמֵינוּ בְּקָרוֹב. אֵל בְּנֵה, אֵל בְּנֵה, בְּנֵה בֵיתְךָ בְּקָרוֹב.

בָּחוּר הוּא, גָּדוֹל הוּא, דָּגוּל הוּא, יִבְנֶה בֵּיתוֹ בְּקָרוֹב, בִּמְהֵרָה בִּמְהֵרָה, בְּיָמֵינוּ בְּקָרוֹב. אֵל בְּנֵה, אֵל בְּנֵה, בְּנֵה בֵיתְךָ בְּקָרוֹב.

הָדוּר הוּא, וָתִיק הוּא, זַכַּאי הוּא, יִבְנֶה בֵּיתוֹ בְּקָרוֹב, בִּמְהֵרָה בִּמְהֵרָה, בְּיָמֵינוּ בְּקָרוֹב. אֵל בְּנֵה, אֵל בְּנֵה, בְּנֵה בֵיתְךָ בְּקָרוֹב.

חָסִיד הוּא, טָהוֹר הוּא, יָחִיד הוּא, יִבְנֶה בֵּיתוֹ בְּקָרוֹב, בִּמְהֵרָה בִּמְהֵרָה, בְּיָמֵינוּ בְּקָרוֹב. אֵל בְּנֵה, אֵל בְּנֵה, בְּנֵה בֵיתְךָ בְּקָרוֹב.

כַּבִּיר הוּא, לָמוּד הוּא, מֶלֶךְ הוּא, יִבְנֶה בֵּיתוֹ בְּקָרוֹב, בִּמְהֵרָה בִּמְהֵרָה, בְּיָמֵינוּ בְּקָרוֹב. אֵל בְּנֵה, אֵל בְּנֵה, בְּנֵה בֵיתְךָ בְּקָרוֹב.

נוֹרָא הוּא, סַגִּיב הוּא, עִזּוּז הוּא, יִבְנֶה בֵּיתוֹ בְּקָרוֹב, בִּמְהֵרָה בִּמְהֵרָה, בְּיָמֵינוּ בְּקָרוֹב. אֵל בְּנֵה, אֵל בְּנֵה, בְּנֵה בֵיתְךָ בְּקָרוֹב.

פּוֹדֶה הוּא, צַדִּיק הוּא, קָדוֹשׁ הוּא, יִבְנֶה בֵּיתוֹ בְּקָרוֹב, בִּמְהֵרָה בִּמְהֵרָה, בְּיָמֵינוּ בְּקָרוֹב. אֵל בְּנֵה, אֵל בְּנֵה, בְּנֵה בֵיתְךָ בְּקָרוֹב.

רַחוּם הוּא, שַׁדַּי הוּא, תַּקִּיף הוּא, יִבְנֶה בֵּיתוֹ בְּקָרוֹב, בִּמְהֵרָה בִּמְהֵרָה, בְּיָמֵינוּ בְּקָרוֹב. אֵל בְּנֵה, אֵל בְּנֵה, בְּנֵה בֵיתְךָ בְּקָרוֹב.

During the height of the devastating famine in Ethiopia, Israel initiates Operation Moses, which brings 15,000 Ethiopian Jews to Israel. In 1990, a 36-hour airlift, Operation Solomon, brings more than 14,000 more. A few thousand Jews remain in Ethiopia, along with a box, reputed to be the Ark of the Covenant, in St. Mary of Zion Church in Aksum.

Almighty is He, may His house be rebuilt soon, in haste, in haste, in our days and soon. God rebuild, God rebuild, rebuild Your house soon.

Ideal is He, titanic is He, noble is He, may His house be rebuilt soon, in haste, in haste, in our days and soon. God rebuild, God rebuild, rebuild Your house soon.

Magnificent is He, venerable is He, pristine is He, may His house be rebuilt soon, in haste, in haste, in our days and soon. God rebuild, God rebuild, rebuild Your house soon.

Benevolent is He, pure is He, unrivaled is He, may His house be rebuilt soon, in haste, in haste, in our days and soon. God rebuild, God rebuild, rebuild Your house soon.

Omnipotent is He, omniscient is He, king is He, may His house be rebuilt soon, in haste, in haste, in our days and soon. God rebuild, God rebuild, rebuild Your house soon.

Awesome is He, soaring is He, supreme is He, may His house be rebuilt soon, in haste, in haste, in our days and soon. God rebuild, God rebuild, rebuild Your house soon.

Redeeming is He, righteous is He, holy is He, may His house be rebuilt soon, in haste, in haste, in our days and soon. God rebuild, God rebuild, rebuild Your house soon.

Compassionate is He, mighty is He, solid is He, may His house be rebuilt soon, in haste, in haste, in our days and soon. God rebuild, God rebuild, rebuild Your house soon.

The critic George Steiner, who left his native France for the United States in 1940, observes: "The survival of the Jews has no authentic parallel in history. Ancient ethnic communities and civilizations no less gifted, no less self-conscious, have perished, many without trace. It is, on the most rational, existential level, difficult to believe that this unique phenomenon of unbroken life, in the face of every destructive agency, is unconnected with the exilic circumstances. Judaism has drawn its uncanny visibility from dispersal, from the adaptive demands made on it by mobility."

ספירת העומר

בָּרוּךְ אַתָּה יהוה, אֱלֹהֵינוּ מֶלֶךְ הָעוֹלָם, אֲשֶׁר קִדְּשָׁנוּ בְּמִצְוֹתָיו, וְצִוָּנוּ עַל סְפִירַת הָעוֹמֶר.

הַיּוֹם יוֹם אֶחָד לָעוֹמֶר.

יְהִי רָצוֹן מִלְּפָנֶיךָ, יהוה אֱלֹהֵינוּ וֵאלֹהֵי אֲבוֹתֵינוּ, שֶׁיִּבָּנֶה בֵּית הַמִּקְדָּשׁ בִּמְהֵרָה בְיָמֵינוּ וְתֵן חֶלְקֵנוּ בְּתוֹרָתֶךָ. וְשָׁם נַעֲבָדְךָ בְּיִרְאָה כִּימֵי עוֹלָם וּכְשָׁנִים קַדְמוֹנִיּוֹת.

רִבּוֹנוֹ שֶׁל עוֹלָם, אַתָּה צִוִּיתָנוּ עַל יְדֵי מֹשֶׁה עַבְדְּךָ לִסְפּוֹר סְפִירַת הָעוֹמֶר, כְּמוֹ שֶׁכָּתַבְתָּ בְּתוֹרָתֶךָ: וּסְפַרְתֶּם לָכֶם מִמָּחֳרַת הַשַּׁבָּת מִיּוֹם הֲבִיאֲכֶם אֶת עוֹמֶר הַתְּנוּפָה שֶׁבַע שַׁבָּתוֹת תְּמִימֹת תִּהְיֶינָה. עַד מִמָּחֳרַת הַשַּׁבָּת הַשְּׁבִיעִית תִּסְפְּרוּ חֲמִשִּׁים יוֹם. וּבְכֵן יְהִי רָצוֹן מִלְּפָנֶיךָ יהוה אֱלֹהֵינוּ וֵאלֹהֵי אֲבוֹתֵינוּ שֶׁבִּזְכוּת סְפִירַת הָעוֹמֶר שֶׁסָּפַרְתִּי הַיּוֹם יְתַקַּן מַה שֶּׁפָּגַמְתִּי בִּסְפִירָה, חֶסֶד שֶׁבְּחֶסֶד, וְאֶטָּהֵר וְאֶתְקַדֵּשׁ בִּקְדֻשָּׁה שֶׁל מַעְלָה, אָמֵן סֶלָה.

1987

During a diplomatic visit to the Soviet Union, Secretary of State George Shultz attends a seder of "refuseniks"—Jews prohibited from emigrating from the USSR.

On the second night only, recite:

Counting the Omer

You are blessed, Lord God-of-Us, King of the Cosmos, who has set us apart with his mitzvot, and instructed us regarding the counting of the Omer.

Today is day one of the Omer.

May it be desirous before You, Lord God-of-Us and God of our fathers, that the Holy Temple be built in haste and in our days—and grant us our share of Your Torah. There we will serve You reverently, as in the days of yore, as in years primeval.

Master of the Universe, You instructed us at the hand of Moses, Your servant, to tally up the Omer, just as You wrote in Your Torah: *From the morrow of the day of rest, on which you bring the waving sheaves of the Omer, you shall tally seven complete weeks. By the morrow of the seventh week, you shall have tallied fifty days.* And thus, may it be desirous before you, Lord God-of-Us and God of our fathers, that on the merit of the Omer that I tallied today, may that which I blemished in the sphere of unconditional kindness be remedied, and may I be purified and sanctified with the holiness of the On-High—an eternal amen.

אֶחָד מִי יוֹדֵעַ?

1989

In response to the hundreds of young Israelis who backpack through the Himalayas after completing their army service, two Lubavitch rabbis travel to Katmandu, Nepal, on the orders of the Lubavitcher rebbe to organize a seder. With help from a local restaurant, they prepare a meal that draws 350 people. The Katmandu Seder becomes an annual event, attracting over 2,000 guests every spring.

1988

Roberta Kalechofsky publishes *Haggadah for the Liberated Lamb*, offering vegetarians an alternative seder plate and a narrative of freedom that includes all creatures.

On both nights, continue:

O ne, one, who knows one?
One, one, I know one.
One is Hashem, in the heavens and the earth.

Two, two, who knows two?
Two, two, I know two.
Two are the tablets of our bond.
And one is Hashem, in the heavens and the earth.

Three, three, who knows three?
Three, three, I know three.
Three are the fathers, Abraham first among.
And two are the tablets of our bond.
And one is Hashem, in the heavens and the earth.

Four, four, who knows four?
Four, four, I know four.
Four are the mothers, whence we come.
And three are the fathers, Abraham first among.
And two are the tablets of our bond.
And one is Hashem, in the heavens and the earth.

Five, five, who knows five?
Five, five, I know five.
Five are the books of the Torah.
And four are the mothers, whence we come.
And three are the fathers, Abraham first among.
And two are the tablets of our bond.
And one is Hashem, in the heavens and the earth.

אֶחָד מִי יוֹדֵעַ? אֶחָד אֲנִי יוֹדֵעַ:
אֶחָד אֱלֹהֵינוּ שֶׁבַּשָּׁמַיִם וּבָאָרֶץ.

שְׁנַיִם מִי יוֹדֵעַ? שְׁנַיִם אֲנִי יוֹדֵעַ:
שְׁנֵי לֻחוֹת הַבְּרִית, אֶחָד אֱלֹהֵינוּ
שֶׁבַּשָּׁמַיִם וּבָאָרֶץ.

שְׁלֹשָׁה מִי יוֹדֵעַ? שְׁלֹשָׁה אֲנִי יוֹדֵעַ:
שְׁלֹשָׁה אָבוֹת, שְׁנֵי לֻחוֹת הַבְּרִית,
אֶחָד אֱלֹהֵינוּ שֶׁבַּשָּׁמַיִם וּבָאָרֶץ.

אַרְבַּע מִי יוֹדֵעַ? אַרְבַּע אֲנִי יוֹדֵעַ:
אַרְבַּע אִמָּהוֹת, שְׁלֹשָׁה אָבוֹת, שְׁנֵי לֻחוֹת
הַבְּרִית, אֶחָד אֱלֹהֵינוּ שֶׁבַּשָּׁמַיִם וּבָאָרֶץ.

חֲמִשָּׁה מִי יוֹדֵעַ? חֲמִשָּׁה אֲנִי יוֹדֵעַ:
חֲמִשָּׁה חֻמְשֵׁי תוֹרָה, אַרְבַּע אִמָּהוֹת,
שְׁלֹשָׁה אָבוֹת, שְׁנֵי לֻחוֹת הַבְּרִית,
אֶחָד אֱלֹהֵינוּ שֶׁבַּשָּׁמַיִם וּבָאָרֶץ.

The world's Jewish population is approximately 12,810,000, or about 0.2% of the total global population. 45.5% of all Jews live in North America, and almost a third live in Israel. The countries of the former USSR still constitute the third-largest Jewish community in the world, but with the fall of the Iron Curtain, hundreds of thousands leave, primarily for Israel.

שִׁשָּׁה מִי יוֹדֵעַ? שִׁשָּׁה אֲנִי יוֹדֵעַ:
שִׁשָּׁה סִדְרֵי מִשְׁנָה, חֲמִשָּׁה חוּמְשֵׁי תּוֹרָה,
אַרְבַּע אִמָּהוֹת, שְׁלֹשָׁה אָבוֹת, שְׁנֵי לֻחוֹת
הַבְּרִית, אֶחָד אֱלֹהֵינוּ שֶׁבַּשָּׁמַיִם וּבָאָרֶץ.

שִׁבְעָה מִי יוֹדֵעַ? שִׁבְעָה אֲנִי יוֹדֵעַ:
שִׁבְעָה יְמֵי שַׁבַּתָּא, שִׁשָּׁה סִדְרֵי מִשְׁנָה,
חֲמִשָּׁה חוּמְשֵׁי תּוֹרָה, אַרְבַּע אִמָּהוֹת,
שְׁלֹשָׁה אָבוֹת, שְׁנֵי לֻחוֹת הַבְּרִית,
אֶחָד אֱלֹהֵינוּ שֶׁבַּשָּׁמַיִם וּבָאָרֶץ.

שְׁמוֹנָה מִי יוֹדֵעַ? שְׁמוֹנָה אֲנִי יוֹדֵעַ:
שְׁמוֹנָה יְמֵי מִילָה, שִׁבְעָה יְמֵי שַׁבַּתָּא,
שִׁשָּׁה סִדְרֵי מִשְׁנָה, חֲמִשָּׁה חוּמְשֵׁי תּוֹרָה,
אַרְבַּע אִמָּהוֹת, שְׁלֹשָׁה אָבוֹת, שְׁנֵי לֻחוֹת
הַבְּרִית, אֶחָד אֱלֹהֵינוּ שֶׁבַּשָּׁמַיִם וּבָאָרֶץ.

תִּשְׁעָה מִי יוֹדֵעַ? תִּשְׁעָה אֲנִי יוֹדֵעַ:
תִּשְׁעָה יַרְחֵי לֵדָה, שְׁמוֹנָה יְמֵי מִילָה,
שִׁבְעָה יְמֵי שַׁבַּתָּא, שִׁשָּׁה סִדְרֵי מִשְׁנָה,
חֲמִשָּׁה חוּמְשֵׁי תּוֹרָה, אַרְבַּע אִמָּהוֹת,
שְׁלֹשָׁה אָבוֹת, שְׁנֵי לֻחוֹת הַבְּרִית,
אֶחָד אֱלֹהֵינוּ שֶׁבַּשָּׁמַיִם וּבָאָרֶץ.

עֲשָׂרָה מִי יוֹדֵעַ? עֲשָׂרָה אֲנִי יוֹדֵעַ:
עֲשָׂרָה דִבְּרַיָּא, תִּשְׁעָה יַרְחֵי לֵדָה,
שְׁמוֹנָה יְמֵי מִילָה, שִׁבְעָה יְמֵי שַׁבַּתָּא, שִׁשָּׁה
סִדְרֵי מִשְׁנָה, חֲמִשָּׁה חוּמְשֵׁי תּוֹרָה, אַרְבַּע
אִמָּהוֹת, שְׁלֹשָׁה אָבוֹת, שְׁנֵי לֻחוֹת הַבְּרִית,
אֶחָד אֱלֹהֵינוּ שֶׁבַּשָּׁמַיִם וּבָאָרֶץ.

Six, six, who knows six?
Six, six, I know six.
Six are the parts of the Mishna.
And five are the books of the Torah.
And four are the mothers, whence we come.
And three are the fathers, Abraham
first among.
And two are the tablets of our bond.
And one is Hashem, in the heavens and
the earth.

Seven, seven, who knows seven?
Seven, seven, I know seven.
Seven days pass with the setting of the
Sabbath sun.
And six are the parts of the Mishna.
And five are the books of the Torah.
And four are the mothers, whence we come.
And three are the fathers, Abraham
first among.
And two are the tablets of our bond.
And one is Hashem, in the heavens and
the earth.

Eight, eight, who knows eight?
Eight, eight, I know eight.
Eight is the day on which the brit is done.
And seven days pass with the setting of the
Sabbath sun.
And six are the parts of the Mishna.
And five are the books of the Torah.
And four are the mothers, whence we come.
And three are the fathers, Abraham
first among.
And two are the tablets of our bond.
And one is Hashem, in the heavens and
the earth.

Nine, nine, who knows nine?
Nine, nine, I know nine.
Nine moons cycle before the baby comes.
And eight is the day on which the brit is done.
And seven days pass with the setting of the
Sabbath sun.
And six are the parts of the Mishna.
And five are the books of the Torah.
And four are the mothers, whence we come.
And three are the fathers, Abraham
first among.
And two are the tablets of our bond.
And one is Hashem, in the heavens and
the earth.

Ten, ten, who knows ten?
Ten, ten, I know ten.
Ten are the commandments, God's will
be done.
And nine moons cycle before the baby comes.
And eight is the day on which the brit is done.
And seven days pass with the setting of the
Sabbath sun.
And six are the parts of the Mishna.
And five are the books of the Torah.
And four are the mothers, whence we come.
And three are the fathers, Abraham
first among.
And two are the tablets of our bond.
And one is Hashem, in the heavens and
the earth.

Dressed in a black
yarmulke in addition
to his traditional
scarlet and golden
robes, the Dalai
Lama is the guest of
honor at a seder that
ends with the call
"Next year in Lhasa."
Guests include
Supreme Court
Justice Stephen
Breyer and Beastie
Boys member Adam
Yauch. The Dalai
Lama pronounces
matzah "very tasty"
and claps along
to "Dayenu."

אֶחָד עָשָׂר מִי יוֹדֵעַ? אֶחָד עָשָׂר אֲנִי יוֹדֵעַ:
אֶחָד עָשָׂר כּוֹכְבַיָּא, עֲשָׂרָה דִבְּרַיָּא, תִּשְׁעָה
יַרְחֵי לֵדָה, שְׁמוֹנָה יְמֵי מִילָה, שִׁבְעָה יְמֵי
שַׁבָּתָא, שִׁשָּׁה סִדְרֵי מִשְׁנָה, חֲמִשָּׁה חוּמְשֵׁי
תוֹרָה, אַרְבַּע אִמָּהוֹת, שְׁלֹשָׁה אָבוֹת, שְׁנֵי לֻחוֹת
הַבְּרִית, אֶחָד אֱלֹהֵינוּ שֶׁבַּשָּׁמַיִם וּבָאָרֶץ.

שְׁנֵים עָשָׂר מִי יוֹדֵעַ? שְׁנֵים עָשָׂר אֲנִי יוֹדֵעַ:
שְׁנֵים עָשָׂר שִׁבְטַיָּא, אֶחָד עָשָׂר כּוֹכְבַיָּא,
עֲשָׂרָה דִבְּרַיָּא, תִּשְׁעָה יַרְחֵי לֵדָה, שְׁמוֹנָה
יְמֵי מִילָה, שִׁבְעָה יְמֵי שַׁבָּתָא, שִׁשָּׁה
סִדְרֵי מִשְׁנָה, חֲמִשָּׁה חוּמְשֵׁי תוֹרָה, אַרְבַּע
אִמָּהוֹת, שְׁלֹשָׁה אָבוֹת, שְׁנֵי לֻחוֹת הַבְּרִית,
אֶחָד אֱלֹהֵינוּ שֶׁבַּשָּׁמַיִם וּבָאָרֶץ.

שְׁלֹשָׁה עָשָׂר מִי יוֹדֵעַ? שְׁלֹשָׁה עָשָׂר
אֲנִי יוֹדֵעַ:
שְׁלֹשָׁה עָשָׂר מִדַּיָּא, שְׁנֵים עָשָׂר שִׁבְטַיָּא,
אֶחָד עָשָׂר כּוֹכְבַיָּא, עֲשָׂרָה דִבְּרַיָּא, תִּשְׁעָה
יַרְחֵי לֵדָה, שְׁמוֹנָה יְמֵי מִילָה, שִׁבְעָה יְמֵי
שַׁבָּתָא, שִׁשָּׁה סִדְרֵי מִשְׁנָה, חֲמִשָּׁה חוּמְשֵׁי
תוֹרָה, אַרְבַּע אִמָּהוֹת, שְׁלֹשָׁה אָבוֹת,
שְׁנֵי לֻחוֹת הַבְּרִית, אֶחָד אֱלֹהֵינוּ
שֶׁבַּשָּׁמַיִם וּבָאָרֶץ.

2001

Metropolitan Tel Aviv
becomes the world's
largest Jewish city,
with 2.5 million Jews.
New York has 1.9
million Jews, or 24%
of the city's total
population. Haifa,
with 655,000 Jews,
and Los Angeles,
with 621,000,
take third and
fourth place.

Eleven, eleven, who knows eleven?

Eleven, eleven, I know eleven.

Eleven are the stars, minus Joseph's one.

And ten are the commandments, God's will
be done.

And nine moons cycle before the baby comes.

And eight is the day on which the brit is done.

And seven days pass with the setting of the
Sabbath sun.

And six are the parts of the Mishna.

And five are the books of the Torah.

And four are the mothers, whence we come.

And three are the fathers, Abraham
first among.

And two are the tablets of our bond.

And one is Hashem, in the heavens and
the earth.

Twelve, twelve, who knows twelve?

Twelve, twelve, I know twelve.

Twelve are the tribes, one each for
Jacob's sons.

And eleven are the stars, minus Joseph's one.

And ten are the commandments, God's will
be done.

And nine moons cycle before the baby comes.

And eight is the day on which the brit is done.

And seven days pass with the setting of the
Sabbath sun.

And six are the parts of the Mishna.

And five are the books of the Torah.

And four are the mothers, whence we come.

And three are the fathers, Abraham
first among.

And two are the tablets of our bond.

And one is Hashem, in the heavens and
the earth.

Thirteen, thirteen, who knows thirteen?

Thirteen, thirteen, I know thirteen.

Thirteen are the traits of God above.

And twelve are the tribes, one each for
Jacob's sons.

And eleven are the stars, minus Joseph's one.

And ten are the commandments, God's will
be done.

And nine moons cycle before the baby comes.

And eight is the day on which the brit is done.

And seven days pass with the setting of the
Sabbath sun.

And six are the parts of the Mishna.

And five are the books of the Torah.

And four are the mothers, whence we come.

And three are the fathers, Abraham
first among.

And two are the tablets of our bond.

And one is Hashem, in the heavens and
the earth.

2005

Just over 80% of the world's 13,034,100 Jews live in the US or Israel: 40.5% in the former, and 40.2% in the latter.

2003

Launch of the Open Source Haggadah, an online software framework that makes it possible for users to compose their own versions of the Haggadah online using a variety of available prayers, translations, commentaries, songs, rituals, and illustrations.

One little goat, one little goat—the one my father bought for two zuzim, one little goat, one little goat.

And here comes the cat that eats up the goat—the one my father bought for two zuzim,

one little goat, one little goat.

And here comes the dog that bites the cat, that ate up the goat—the one my father bought for two zuzim,

one little goat, one little goat.

And here comes the staff that beats up the dog, that bit the cat, that ate up the goat—the one my father bought for two zuzim,

one little goat, one little goat.

And here comes the fire that burns up the staff, that beat up the dog, that bit the cat, that ate up the goat—the one my father bought for two zuzim,

one little goat, one little goat.

חַד גַּדְיָא, חַד גַּדְיָא.

דְּזַבִּין אַבָּא בִּתְרֵי זוּזֵי, חַד גַּדְיָא חַד גַּדְיָא.

וַאֲתָא שׁוּנְרָא וְאָכַל לְגַדְיָא,

דְּזַבִּין אַבָּא בִּתְרֵי זוּזֵי, חַד גַּדְיָא חַד גַּדְיָא.

וַאֲתָא כַלְבָּא וְנָשַׁךְ לְשׁוּנְרָא

דְּאָכַל לְגַדְיָא,

דְּזַבִּין אַבָּא בִּתְרֵי זוּזֵי, חַד גַּדְיָא חַד גַּדְיָא.

וַאֲתָא חוּטְרָא וְהִכָּה לְכַלְבָּא

דְּנָשַׁךְ לְשׁוּנְרָא דְּאָכַל לְגַדְיָא,

דְּזַבִּין אַבָּא בִּתְרֵי זוּזֵי, חַד גַּדְיָא חַד גַּדְיָא.

וַאֲתָא נוּרָא וְשָׂרַף לְחוּטְרָא,

דְּהִכָּה לְכַלְבָּא דְּנָשַׁךְ לְשׁוּנְרָא

דְּאָכַל לְגַדְיָא,

דְּזַבִּין אַבָּא בִּתְרֵי זוּזֵי, חַד גַּדְיָא חַד גַּדְיָא.

2006

The Center for Cultural Judaism publishes *The Liberated Haggadah*, a seder for those who identify as cultural, secular, and humanistic Jews.

וְאָתָא מַיָּא וְכָבָה לְנוּרָא

דְּשָׂרַף לְחוּטְרָא, דְּהִכָּה לְכַלְבָּא,

דְּנָשַׁךְ לְשׁוּנְרָא דְּאָכַל לְגַדְיָא,

דְּזַבִּין אַבָּא בִּתְרֵי זוּזֵי, חַד גַּדְיָא חַד גַּדְיָא.

וְאָתָא תוֹרָא וְשָׁתָה לְמַיָּא

דְּכָבָה לְנוּרָא, דְּשָׂרַף לְחוּטְרָא, דְּהִכָּה

לְכַלְבָּא, דְּנָשַׁךְ לְשׁוּנְרָא דְּאָכַל לְגַדְיָא,

דְּזַבִּין אַבָּא בִּתְרֵי זוּזֵי, חַד גַּדְיָא חַד גַּדְיָא.

וְאָתָא הַשּׁוֹחֵט וְשָׁחַט לְתוֹרָא

דְּשָׁתָה לְמַיָּא, דְּכָבָה לְנוּרָא,

דְּשָׂרַף לְחוּטְרָא, דְּהִכָּה לְכַלְבָּא, דְּנָשַׁךְ

לְשׁוּנְרָא דְּאָכַל לְגַדְיָא,

דְּזַבִּין אַבָּא בִּתְרֵי זוּזֵי, חַד גַּדְיָא חַד גַּדְיָא.

וְאָתָא מַלְאַךְ הַמָּוֶת וְשָׁחַט לְשׁוֹחֵט

דְּשָׁחַט לְתוֹרָא, דְּשָׁתָה לְמַיָּא, דְּכָבָה

לְנוּרָא, דְּשָׂרַף לְחוּטְרָא, דְּהִכָּה לְכַלְבָּא,

דְּנָשַׁךְ לְשׁוּנְרָא דְּאָכַל לְגַדְיָא,

דְּזַבִּין אַבָּא בִּתְרֵי זוּזֵי, חַד גַּדְיָא חַד גַּדְיָא.

וְאָתָא הַקָּדוֹשׁ בָּרוּךְ הוּא וְשָׁחַט

לְמַלְאַךְ הַמָּוֶת, דְּשָׁחַט לְשׁוֹחֵט דְּשָׁחַט

לְתוֹרָא, דְּשָׁתָה לְמַיָּא, דְּכָבָה לְנוּרָא,

דְּשָׂרַף לְחוּטְרָא, דְּהִכָּה לְכַלְבָּא, דְּנָשַׁךְ

לְשׁוּנְרָא דְּאָכַל לְגַדְיָא,

דְּזַבִּין אַבָּא בִּתְרֵי זוּזֵי, חַד גַּדְיָא חַד גַּדְיָא.

2007

Publication of the
first Haggadah
designed for Jewish
Buddhists.

2007

At St. Catherine's
Monastery, built
by the Emperor
Justinian in the 6th
century at the foot
of what might have
been Mount Sinai,
at the site where
Moses might have
seen the Burning
Bush, monks still
tend what is reputed
to be the original—a
scraggy Colutea
istria with bright
yellow flowers.

And here comes the water that puts out the fire, that burned up the staff, that beat up the dog, that bit the cat, that ate up the goat—the one my father bought for two zuzim,

one little goat, one little goat.

And here comes the ox that drinks up the water, that put out the fire, that burned up the staff, that beat up the dog, that bit the cat, that ate up the goat—the one my father bought for two zuzim,

one little goat, one little goat.

And here comes the butcher who slaughters the ox, that drank up the water, that put out the fire, that burned up the staff, that beat up the dog, that bit the cat, that ate up the goat—the one my father bought for two zuzim,

one little goat, one little goat.

And here comes the Angel of Death, who butchers the butcher, who slaughtered the ox, that drank up the water, that put out the fire, that burned up the staff, that beat up the dog, that bit the cat, that ate up the goat—the one my father bought for two zuzim,

one little goat, one little goat.

And here comes the Holy One, blessed is He, who slits the throat of the Angel of Death, who butchered the butcher, who slaughtered the ox, that drank up the water, that put out the fire, that burned up the staff, that beat up the dog, that bit the cat, that ate up the goat—the one my father bought for two zuzim,

one little goat, one little goat.

The rabbi and his disciples were reclining together in B'nai Prague, and they went on discussing "Chad Gadya" all night long.

"What is the goat?" he asked. "It is the Holy Temple, where the sacrifice of the animal had been offered," answered a disciple. "And every family was required to pay to the priests the price of two zuzim as their atonement."

"Then why," asked another, "must the dog be punished for biting the cat that ate the goat? Is it not justified that the destroyers of the Holy Temple be punished?"

"It is because the destroyers of the destroyers are themselves full of sin," answered one. "No," said another. "The dog is as innocent as the goat. This is why the staff that beat the dog is burned." "But the fire that burned the staff is itself quenched by the water," objected the first student, "from which we learn that all are deserving of punishment until the day of the final redemption." "Not all merit punishment," demurred another, "but the innocent will suffer along with the guilty until the arrival of the Messiah, when the Angel of Death will himself be destroyed by God, as it is written in the last stanza." "Yes," said another, "the path was determined from the beginning of time! And this is the reason we go back to the beginning and repeat each verse of the song!"

At daybreak, they noticed that their rabbi had long been silent, and that now he was weeping. "He weeps with joy, because his students discuss Torah until the moment for dawn Shema!" they murmured. But when he looked up they saw that his face was anguished, and understanding stopped their words. All night long they had debated the theological meaning of suffering, citing laws and commentaries, and never once had they groaned aloud for the sufferers. "What is the goat?" their rabbi asked them again. "What is the goat?"

"Chad Gadya" begins with "one little goat" and ends with the One God. On the path from the one to the other, there are no shortcuts. We first encounter the cat before we encounter the dog before we encounter the staff and so on. Even the Angel of Death must wait his turn. Even God.

"Chad Gadya" teaches us that even a small act of violence can lead all the way to God. So, too, can a small act of love....For, as Franz Rosenzweig explains in *The Star of Redemption*, his masterpiece of Jewish theology, "there is no act of neighborly love that falls in the void...because of the unbroken interconnectedness of all objects.." In this way, the commandment to "love your neighbor like yourself" (Leviticus 19:18) is intimately and profoundly linked to the commandment to "love the Lord your God with all your heart, and all your soul, and all your might" (Deuteronomy 6:5).

In Judaism—as in "Chad Gadya"—the path to God is marked by small steps rather than giant leaps. We cannot reach God through the grandest gesture, yet we cannot avoid reaching him through the humblest act.

"Chad Gadya"

Someone's father purchases a goat, and this goat starts a cavalcade of anguish and gluttony, with animals, objects, people, and supernatural beings all dragged into the all-consuming whirlpool of the song. The entire universe changes, and it is all because of one goat, and it has been this way since the beginning of time, in every story that has ever been told. In the story of Passover, for example, if Moses had not been rescued from his basket in the reeds, the Jewish people might still be slaves in Egypt, so the infant Moses can be said to be a goat. If your parents had never met, then there might be an uglier, crueler person sitting at the Passover table, instead of your own charming self, so your parents are goats. Every person in the world, and every action each person takes, is a goat, accumulating cats and dogs and staffs and fires and all of the joy and terror that makes up the stuff of the universe. You are a goat, and when you wake up in the morning, that is a goat, and eating breakfast is a goat, and all the goats all over the world are goating and goating and goating, all the time wondering if the goat they are and the goats they are goating are the right goat or the wrong goat, which is why the world often seems as stubborn as a goat, as ravenous as a goat, as loud as a goat, as grumpy as a goat, as quick and jumpy and frisky and soft and woolly and horny and tally as a goat—until the world itself seems to be a goat, made up of countless other goats, and watched over by some enormous, all-seeing goat who created all this goating in its image.

Playground

This is a highly amusing song with awesome meaning. If you accept the political interpretation of "Chad Gadya," that the kid represents the Jewish people, and that the cat plays the part of Assyria, and Rome the ox, and so on, then the message of "Chad Gadya" is nothing less than the message of the seder itself: It may seem that persecution will last forever, but it will not—and it will be the righteous God who brings about its end. "Chad Gadya" also teaches us the importance of small acts. Follow the song all the way through: One little goat is ultimately responsible for the smiting of the Angel of Death by God. That's some goat.

Most great movements for change start with small acts by anonymous people (think Shifra and Puah, for example). The Arab Spring is a good example from the current day. In a single year, despots in several Arab countries—including, it is worth noting, the despot referred to by his unhappy Egyptian subjects as Pharaoh—were overthrown in popular uprisings. And how did this great wave of unrest start? It started because a vegetable vendor in an out-of-the-way Tunisian village, oppressed by an uncaring and rapacious government, burnt himself alive to protest his treatment. His death enraged all of Tunisia, and that rage spread to Libya, Egypt, and beyond.

The power of a single human being is awesome, in part because so few individual acts occur in a vacuum. We all look to others for leadership, for positive examples. Which means that we have within us the power to be that example. We all have within us the power to spark revolutions, through the lives we choose to lead. And it is our choice! Judaism, Jonathan Sacks wrote, "is the religion of the free human being freely responding to the God of freedom." If a mere goat can bring about the smiting of the Angel of Death, just imagine what you, a free person, could do, just by responding to the God of freedom.

Nation

When I began translating this Haggadah, it quickly became clear that the best way to engage with a traditional text was in a traditional form. By the time I'd finished, I'd spent countless hours studying in *hevruta*—arguing the text head to head, word by word, with a study partner. This was seminal not only to the translation, but to the shape of the liturgy itself. I would like to acknowledge the joyous process of working with, and the massive contribution made by, Baruch Thaler: my *hevruta*, my teacher, my friend. I'd also like to thank Marc Platt, who so generously made it possible for me to devote myself to this project over these last years.

Nathan Englander

Jews have been designing Haggadahs for more than one hundred generations. Deliberately, or not, these designs have inevitably reflected the time in which they were made. The notion behind the design of this book was to merge, visually, the history of the Jewish nation with the traditional text of the Haggadah. Toward that end, the letterforms on each page reflect those used in the period reflected in the timeline at the top of the page. In this way, the book is a graphic record of Jewish history.

This Haggadah would not have been possible without the generosity of Marc Platt, who made it possible for me to work exclusively on this project. I would also like to thank my dedicated design assistant, Nirit Pe'er.

Oded Ezer

You can use these pages to
write your name, the place you
celebrated Passover, the year,
and any important memories.
Over time, this book will become
a living record of its use.